# IS YOUR CHILD ANGRY?

It's not always easy to recognize anger in children. This powerful emotion can take many forms: tantrums in toddlers, hostility and sarcasm in adolescents—or in some cases, depression, compulsiveness, addiction, and other problem behaviors. *When Kids Are Mad, Not Bad* will tell you . . .

- How children use anger to communicate
- What makes children angry
- How age, gender, and background can affect a child's expression of anger
- The right and wrong ways to handle children's anger
- The dangers of mishandling anger
- How increased understanding of anger ensures healthy development—and strengthens the bond between parent and child

# WHEN KIDS ARE MAD,

PRAISE FOR
# WHEN KIDS ARE MAD, NOT BAD

"All children get mad sometimes and express this feeling in different ways. But many parents haven't the foggiest notion why this happens. Their ignorance drives them to discharge their own anxiety, propelling both parent and child into an implacable duct of anger, time and time again.

"So three cheers for Dr. Paul, who spells it all out in this essential book for one of the most difficult and draining of parental dilemmas. While this book has been written for adults, Dr. Paul's gentle approach and clearly described vignettes make the book readable by children and teenagers as well. Everyone can profit by knowing more about anger, either in oneself or in others. In *When Kids Are Mad, Not Bad*, one learns without fanfare or jargon about the basic elements of anger and how it can be responded to in constructive ways."

—Helen DeRosis, M.D., Clinical Professor of Psychiatry, New York University School of Medicine, Author of *Parent Power Child Power*, *The Book of Hope*, and *Women and Anxiety*

# When Kids Are Mad, Not Bad

*A Guide to Recognizing and Handling Children's Anger*

## HENRY A. PAUL, M.D.

BERKLEY BOOKS, NEW YORK

WHEN KIDS ARE MAD, NOT BAD

A Berkley Book / published by arrangement with
the author

PRINTING HISTORY
Berkley edition / March 1995

ISBN: 0-425-14648-0

BERKLEY®
Berkley Books are published by The Berkley Publishing Group,
200 Madison Avenue, New York, New York 10016.
BERKLEY and the "B" design
are trademarks belonging to Berkley Publishing Corporation.

PRINTED IN THE UNITED STATES OF AMERICA

10  9  8  7  6  5  4

This book is dedicated to my parents, Evelyn and Milton Paul; my wife, Carol; my children, Lila and Jonathan; and the many patients and students from whom I have learned the most.

I would like to acknowledge the persistent help and optimism of Charlotte Sheedy, the assistance of Linda Crawford, and the cheerful, intelligent, and constructive attitude of my editor, Heather Jackson.

# CONTENTS

# Introduction

Anger is a difficult emotion for many of us. We wonder if we should express it, how hurtful it is, if we express anger appropriately, and if it is normal. Many of these same questions occur when it comes to understanding a youngster's anger. Should we try to control children's angry feelings? Should we encourage kids to vent their anger? Are angry feelings signs of underlying problems in our children? Anger generates a lot of confusion.

In my work as a psychiatrist, I've become keenly aware of the many problems parents have with understanding and managing anger. They have shown a great hunger for straightforward knowledge about anger. In a culture that has great ambivalence about angry feelings and treats them with marked inconsistency, they want guidelines for handling this largely misunderstood emotion.

Anger problems can begin in the earliest days of our lives, and healthy anger management can begin there also. I've written this book in the hope that anyone who deals with children—especially parents, but also those who work with children such as teachers, clergy, coaches, and counsellors—can glean a deeper understanding of children's anger and learn about some helpful tools for dealing with it.

The angry feelings our children exhibit don't mean they're "bad," and these feelings needn't be frightening to parents. Anger is a natural, healthy, appropriate, life-enhancing emotion. Also, it is a great communicator—often the only one children have—to convey their distress. It is a signal that they need help to overcome predictable developmental hurdles, as well as the strains and stresses that come up in their relationships with others. Whatever the cause, the concerned adult should try to understand the source of the anger and attempt to aid the child in the most appropriate manner. This constructive interaction is important to normal development. When adults understand this, they handle their children's anger in a way that opens the door to healthy growth.

Adults may have problems seeing anger as a natural feeling, and there are many reasons why they have this prejudice. Usually, parents' beliefs about anger emanate from their own past. Having had their own angry feelings mishandled, these adults often repeat the same mistakes with their children. When this happens over a prolonged period of time, the stage is set for what I call the "anger metamorphosis"—an insidious process that results in transforming a child's anger into a more malignant force, which in turn fosters the development of a host of different psychiatric problems—the legacies of mishandled anger.

My hope is that this book will serve as a starting point for the exploration of the myriad ways that anger appears in all of our lives and the powerful effects—both positive and negative—that this feeling exerts on parent-child relations. Anger is normal, healthy, and instructive—let's teach our children the importance of its natural expression and do away with the legacies its mishandling can bring.

# PART ONE

# Anger, the Great Communicator

# CHAPTER ONE

# What Is Anger?

Children learn about anger from us, the adults in their world. Because of our own confusion and anxiety about this feeling, we frequently teach our children that anger is a "bad" feeling, one to be avoided, denied, or covered up. There are probably as many taboos about anger in our culture as there were about sex in Victorian society.

The questions about anger that concerned parents, patients, and friends commonly ask me are a good indicator to our bewilderment and apprehension.

*"My child's angry. Will he ever be happy?"*

*"I'm so angry. Do you think there's a chance I could lose control and kill my child?"*

*"Is my daughter's anger a sign that she's very sick?"*

*"Can you teach my son to express his anger?"*

*"Will my screaming ruin my child?"*

*"Do you think my angry son will become an assassin?"*

# 8  ANGER, THE GREAT COMMUNICATOR

*"Isn't competing a sign that my child's angry?"*
*"Will my kids love me if I get angry?"*

What exactly is this feeling that gives us so much trouble? The dictionary defines anger as a sense of displeasure or distress caused by feelings of powerlessness or helplessness. Similar to frustration, it can run the gamut from mild irritation to rage and fury.

I would add to this basic definition that anger is a perfectly normal feeling. It is as natural as joy, love, sorrow, disappointment, excitement, or any other emotion. Like them, it's a vital part of being human, and it is as life-enhancing as more pleasant feelings. Whether we're aware of it or not, most of us probably experience anger every day. So do our kids, from the very beginning of life.

As children grow and develop, they are presented each day with new challenges, and anger is a frequent and appropriate response to many of these obstacles. When learning how to do new things, children often don't do them perfectly the first time. They're more likely, in fact, to fall on their faces.

When toddlers are learning to walk, for example, this happens quite literally. When youngsters are older—perhaps approaching their first boy-girl party, feeling tongue-tied and awkward—the fall may be metaphorical. The child, quite naturally, experiences a sense of helplessness in either circumstance. Anger in response to helplessness is as common as waking and sleeping.

Children also respond angrily when interactions

with other people cause them to feel frustrated. They may get mad when their needs aren't met immediately, when someone's insensitive to those needs, or when their sense of well-being is threatened in any number of ways. Again, a feeling of helplessness produces anger, which is perfectly normal. A child who never seems angry, in fact, is a greater cause for concern than one who expresses anger more frequently and demonstratively.

For all of us—adults and children—anger is also a good general indicator of our psychological equilibrium. Do we feel balanced, imbued with a sense of stability, competent? Or do we feel unstable, a bit out of control, perhaps in need of help? Angry feelings communicate this distress and indicate that attention is needed. Generally, once the situation is addressed, our equilibrium returns, and our anger diminishes.

Children continually find themselves in situations they haven't yet learned how, or aren't yet equipped, to handle. They're bound to feel out of control and powerless when this happens. For them, especially, anger is essential to their well-being. It signals their need for help and hopefully calls forth aid.

Kids show their anger in different ways, depending on a number of factors, but one thing is invariably true about children's expression of anger: If they are allowed to, they show it clearly and directly, from infancy right through to adolescence. Each of the following examples illustrates healthy anger expression in the many phases of childhood development.

# 10  ANGER, THE GREAT COMMUNICATOR

*Mary, a three-month-old infant, screamed each time her mother put her in her crib after eating. With her arms and legs thrashing and a scowl on her face, she was unmistakably angry. Her mother discovered that she simply had to pick up Mary and walk with her for five minutes after each meal for the cries to stop. Mary needed that time to separate gradually from her mother and for the digestive process to begin smoothly.*

*At eleven months, Andre was just beginning to walk on his own. After pulling himself up on the arm of a chair, he'd take two big steps, then fall with a thump on his bottom and begin crying and pounding the floor with his hands. This display of angry feelings disappeared when Andre's sensitive six-year-old brother took hold of Andre's hand and helped him to walk at least another few steps.*

*Susan, a three-year-old, never missed a chance to try piling up her older sister's cardboard blocks. When the stacks grew too high and toppled over, Susan dissolved in tears and hit the blocks or threw them against the wall. Her mother soon realized that Susan's constructions had a better chance of succeeding with fewer and smaller wooden blocks. This proved to be the key to better building, and Susan's anger subsided.*

*Third-grader Charlie wanted desperately to join his buddies in a baseball game at the playground, but it was getting dark and his mother said no. Immediately, Charlie turned on his little sister, belittling her and making unkind remarks. Told to go to his room, he went off pouting. Later on, his mother had a chance to explain that there were limits to what was safe and allowable. She reassured Charlie that his angry behavior was understandable, but that abusing someone else wouldn't be permitted. Also, she reminded him there'd be baseball the next day.*

*Fifteen-year-old John went directly to his room when he came home from school, clapped on his headphones, and lay on the bed. When his mother knocked to announce dinner, he greeted her with a look of exaggerated annoyance, as though she'd interrupted an important private meeting. He wasn't eating, he said, and told her to get out of the room. When she asked what was bothering him, he answered, "You are, and I really wish you'd leave me alone." She did. A few hours later, when he entered the living room looking very sad, he was ready to talk about being rejected for a spot on the school soccer team.*

Anger is a great communicator. It alerts us to our children's needs, both physical and emotional. Without expressions of angry feelings, we parents and other caretakers might remain in the dark as to our children's feelings. If an infant didn't wail angrily, would we know that she was hungry, too warm or too cold, frightened, or uncomfortable in some other way? Without a temper tantrum, would we understand that a toddler is distressed to find himself in a big world without the skills he sees in the adults around him? A preschooler separated from her mother and plunked down in an environment where she's not so special may only show her concern by arguing. Older children frequently indicate their various worries regarding school, friendships, siblings, dating, athletics, and so on by exhibiting angry feelings. Would we recognize our own unintended little slights to our children if their anger didn't tip us off?

## REMEMBER THESE ESSENTIAL CHARACTERISTICS OF ANGER

- It's nearly always triggered by a sense of helplessness.
- It's usually understandable, if not immediately, then after a short time of observation.
- Its expression varies with the age and the personality of the particular child.
- Anger disappears when the sense of helplessness abates.
- The angry episode leaves no lasting damage.

- Since feelings of helplessness are often temporary, and natural anger, freely expressed, can elicit help, we should view anger as a constructive feeling, not a destructive one.

# CHAPTER TWO

# Why We Mishandle Children's Anger

When our children are mad, it seldom poses insurmountable problems for most of us. We may find it temporarily disconcerting, but we manage to deal with our own discomfort in a constructive fashion. We make our child's need the first priority, locating the source of her distress and handling her anger in a constructive way, easing the sense of helplessness that's causing the anger in the first place. Although few of us do this perfectly, and we all experience some bad moments with an angry child, for the most part, we succeed. Gradually, we learn with and from our child about what causes her anger, how it is expressed, and how she responds to help. On the whole, the great majority of us are adequate parents, and as a result, our children grow up without serious and lingering anger problems.

For some of us, though, angry children are far more troublesome and disturbing, and when this is true, there is the risk of mishandling our child's anger. This mishandling of anger can become a major, perhaps the primary source of psychological, social, and behavioral difficulties for these children and their problems can continue into adulthood.

The reasons and ways we mishandle anger are wide-ranging. They may be conscious and apparent, which makes them easier to correct, or unconscious and below the surface, which makes it somewhat more difficult. One thing's fairly certain: You can reverse the mishandling of anger if you become aware of your own position regarding this feeling. This means you must seriously examine your past and present attitudes and behaviors with regard to anger, and you must make an effort to change. As we become more knowledgeable, tolerant, and understanding about our own attitudes toward anger, the chances of mishandling this feeling with our children diminishes.

As I have mentioned before, I am convinced that there are ample opportunities all along the road to legacy formation where we can stop its progression by altering our own behaviors. I have seen positive results many times, even in cases where people felt they couldn't understand the problem or change their ways.

As you read about whys, hows, and methods of mishandling anger, please keep in mind that it is certain that you will see some aspect of yourself in these pages. There is no reason for alarm or panic. After all, being human entails many less-than-perfect qualities. I would be most disturbed, in fact, by someone who denied a connection or a relatedness to any of these issues.

Actually, you will probably see at least traces of yourself, if not more, in more than one area. Issues that cause us trouble with angry children and some of the methods we use in mishandling anger are often multiple and have overlapping qualities.

The best way for you to approach this section is to see the following categories as extremes of common, everyday characteristics and to realize that it is as rare to meet someone without a trace of these characteristics as it is to meet someone who totally fits the category's description.

## COMMON REASONS FOR MISHANDLING ANGER

I have broken down the reasons adults have trouble in handling childrens' anger into the following categories:

- Poor anger education
- Anger confusion
- Fear of spoiling a child
- Excessive need for control
- Unconscious identification with the angry child
- Perfectionism
- Poor self-image
- Personality traits such as dependency, egocentric-

ity, martyrdom, revengefulness, and knowing everything

## Poor Anger Education

Poor anger education is the most common reason for mishandling anger. A person with a poor anger education has never fully learned that anger is a natural feeling, as normal as any of the other emotions that we commonly experience. He may, in fact, have been taught the opposite.

As children, all of us mimic the behavior of the important figures in our lives. If they or their culture had trouble dealing with anger, we may learn similar, unproductive ways of handling it—we "inherit" these biases. Intolerance for anger is frequently passed on in this way from generation to generation.

Unfortunately, when we don't understand that anger is normal, indeed inevitable, we're apt to make judgments about it that are often quite extreme. We may see it, among other things, as evil, bad, malignant, rude, impolite, potentially explosive, a precursor of psychopathology, or even a sign of the devil's influence. People who view anger in any of these ways generally feel that children should be seen and not heard. If they're heard, after all, what they say might be wicked, impolite, disruptive, not nice, subversive, or frightening.

People who have been raised to disapprove of anger have usually also been taught not to probe their attitudes or question too closely their feelings about anger. They probably haven't struggled through the trial and error process of learning about angry feelings and finally arriving at their own conclusions and beliefs. They simply feel that they know what's right and what's wrong and would probably be surprised to discover that others have ideas about anger that are different from theirs.

Strictness is often the rule with parents who have had a poor anger education. Certainly, there are times during child rearing when a firm hand is appropriate, but extreme strictness is knee-jerk, automatic, and unexamined. Parents who practice it haven't chosen severe and exacting treatment because it's a well-considered approach that fits a particular child. They've adopted strictness as a blanket policy, no matter what the circumstances, no matter who the individual.

A household that doesn't allow anger is unlikely to be emotionally open in other respects, and commonly, the atmosphere is rather stilted and lacking in vitality. When people are forced to suppress one emotion, other feelings become casualties as well. It's hard to be selective once we begin closing doors to our emotions. They're not items on a menu, we can't order some and pass on others.

*I was once consulted about a seven-year-old, Sarah, who, her mother said, had "all sorts of behavior problems" at home. Sarah was described as "rude, talking back a great deal, and sloppy" in the way she cared for her room and her pos-*

*sessions. Curiously, Sarah's school considered her an ideal student who virtually never misbehaved.*

*Her mother was a well-meaning woman who had a long list of rather rigid ideas about how a child should behave and was quite inflexible about these, especially regarding her intolerance of anger. In addition, her particular rules didn't fit Sarah's temperament, nor were they relevant to her stage of development. Sarah was an easygoing, normal child and certainly much too young to be able to live within some of the rules set by her mother. When I began working toward getting the mother to relax these rules, especially her intolerance of anger, she was skeptical, to say the least. As Sarah's mother courageously tried to become more tolerant, Sarah's "behavior problems" diminished.*

Fortunately, a poor anger education is not necessarily a deep-rooted problem. What's been learned can be unlearned as well. People with poor anger educations often succeed in changing their attitudes about this emotion when they learn new ways to approach it.

## Anger Confusion

We get mixed messages from our culture, which glorifies war, violence, and deadly serious athletic competition. At the same time, we glorify the absence of agression in our espousal of humility, the golden rule, brotherly love, and turning the other cheek. From reading the cultural signs, how could we possibly tell if anger is desirable or not?

I've also noted that confusion about anger exists even among the experts. One book may argue the case against expressing anger; the other may advocate expressing it at all times. The same expert may even expound conflicting opinions about the expression of anger.

To debate such matters is fine, and certainly there's room for many views and even for changing one's views based on new experiences and insights. It's also a measure of how much confusion exists on the subject. We simply don't argue about other feelings the way we do about anger, nor are we as confused about them.

## Fear of Spoiling a Child

Related to a poor anger education and to anger confusion, fear of spoiling a child equates an angry child with a demanding and unruly one. A parent who views anger this way fears that such a child will govern the household, run roughshod over everyone in it, fail to learn self-control, and end up overindulged and unable to cope with a world that won't cater to his every whim. Sometimes, acting on this fear, the parent feels obliged to bend over backward in the other direction, withholding from the child the perfectly normal gratification of certain needs.

Although usually not a very serious problem, sometimes this attitude has certain complicated roots stemming from deep-seated, complex, unconscious feelings of having been neglected oneself. When this is the case, it can be very difficult to change. Fortunately, most of the people I've encountered who fear spoiling their child have responded well to anger education and discussion of their own pasts.

*A woman once told me how exasperated she was that her ten-year-old son didn't want to go to sleep at the designated hour of 8:30 P.M. He constantly came up with new ways of avoiding and resisting his bedtime. She couldn't understand where the anger was coming from because she felt—appropriately—that she was a caring person, who'd done a good job as a mother.*

*She then confided that even she felt that 8:30 was too early a bedtime for a ten-year-old. Still, given all his anger, now she was afraid to back down lest her son think "he could get his own way with such tactics." She thought she'd be setting the stage for spoiling her child—echoes of her own parents' worries when raising her.*

This woman was amenable to anger education and was able to reformulate her own expectations. She came to understand that her fear of spoiling her child could actually perpetuate his anger and, ironically, spoil his ability to handle anger appropriately because of constant frustration and lack of receptivity on her part. This was quite different from what she'd envisaged: a tyrant unleashed because he'd gotten his way by wielding his anger against her.

## Need for Excessive Control

An excessive need for control can lead to mishandling a child's anger. Most of us, naturally, strive for some degree of stability and calm in our lives, but there are some of us for whom these reasonable goals have hardened into an imperative. We sometimes give these people the slang label of "control freaks." Anger represents a major disruptive force for them, since it nearly always makes waves to one degree or another.

This need for control may stem from a number of individual reasons but is often rationalized by equating spontaneity with catastrophe. People who are wedded to such rigid control secretly fear that, given the least bit of freedom, they would be at the mercy of their own impulses. They fear losing control over their own anger and destructively acting out. They may also fear their sexual feelings and/or their urges to eat, spend money, gamble, use drugs, and drink, among other things.

Suspecting such inner chaos, they take great pains to create an orderly surface, clamping down on expression in general, frequently becoming compulsive about a number of things, such as household chores, appointments, nutrition, progress in their children's development and, especially, their children's behavior. Anger, as much as anything else, threatens to upset their equilibrium, although, ironically, they're often the angriest of people. They may live, in fact, on the verge of an angry panic which, of course, breaks out whenever things don't go as planned.

## Unconscious Identification with an Angry Child

Seeing some aspects of ourselves in our child is perfectly normal. Many of us retain painful memories of our pasts—when we were treated poorly, when we suffered, when we were in pain, when we were angry, and when this feeling was mishandled in one way or another. Often these memories are not in our conscious awareness. Because of all the associated pain, it's easier not to focus on them. When we see a normal angry child, we may automatically be reminded of who we were as children—helpless and angry—and may then exaggerate or distort the anger we see in the child because of our own memories of personal suffering. These revived painful memories, conscious or not, make it extremely difficult to act constructively as parents at these times. Either we see our child as overly angry (as we may have been) and overreact, or we feel too helpless (like we did as children) to do much for the child.

In extreme cases, the confusion between where we leave off and the child begins is so great that anger creates huge difficulties from day one. Often, the possibility of child abuse or neglect exists in these cases.

Even when the situation I've described isn't extreme, however, one can see and feel how difficult it is for such a parent. The innocent, angry child dredges up memories and conflicts and revives in the parent the feelings of a painful period in the past. It's bound to be difficult to handle the child's anger constructively under these circumstances.

Interestingly, another result of overidentification with a child can lead to mishandling anger in a different way. The parent, unknowingly, and for his own needs, may actually stimulate anger in a child. This way, the parent's anger gets acted out by someone else.

*A father once described to me how upset he was that his son was constantly fighting with other members of the neighborhood boys' club. In fact, this child was often in hot water and had a developing reputation as a troublemaker and a kid to stay away from. But the look on the father's face didn't reflect the worry he said he felt about this situation. It told a quite different story. I could tell that he relished his son's fighting and waited eagerly for daily reports from the front.*

*After gathering some history, I learned that the father had considered himself a "chicken" in childhood fights. At the same time, he felt that physical fights were beneath him. Obviously, he'd had a long-standing conflict in this regard and his son's anger called the unconscious conflict into play without the father even realizing it.*

*His response indicated both his confusion and his identification with his son. He chastised the boy for fighting at the same time as he stimulated his aggression, a distinctly mixed message. What the boy heard primarily was that his father's childhood intimidation still had to be overcome; he took it upon himself to do this and thus to heal his father's earlier wounds.*

## Perfectionism

Perfectionistic people make excessive demands on themselves. They are nearly always in a state of strife because, being imperfectly human, they're doomed to fall short of the impossibly high goals they've set. Of course this sense of failure, of not quite making it, takes a great toll on their everyday functioning. Never fully succeeding, never quite measuring up in their own estimation, these people don't feel entitled to reward themselves for a job well done. They are often irritable, dissatisfied, and angry.

Because looking inward holds no satisfaction, they often shift their focus to the external world, including their children. They begin to count on others to boost their ego, to make them feel good about themselves, to furnish them with rewards. Over time, this becomes an ingrained pattern, and they end up highly dependent upon other people to provide the satisfaction that lies beyond their grasp. Of course, most children are busy with their own growth and development, and they could not satisfy a perfectionist, anyway. An angry child presents a greater problem for such beleaguered souls. As the perfectionist gazes outward, seeking rewards or at least a sense of satisfaction—in the form of a compliment, a sign of affection, gratitude, or appreciation—instead, a dark cloud is encountered. There is a scowling, screaming, or sulking child. Such a parent can only understand displays like these as more disapproval, more criticism, further failure. The parent adds self-condemnation to what he perceives as negative judgments from the outside as well. The burden grows heavier. The child's anger and the parent's anger bounce back and forth, feeding off each other, and nothing constructive can result.

## Poor Self-Image

This common culprit in the mishandling of children's anger often accompanies perfectionism and chronic self-criticism. The sources of low self-esteem are, of course, varied and highly individual, but parents who feel they're less than able and not quite good enough commonly turn to their kids to make them feel better about themselves.

In these circumstances, the child is not free to be himself. He is an extension of the parent, a stand-in, a vehicle for lifting the parent's low self-esteem. How the child performs and behaves may become synonymous in the parent's mind with the way others see the parent. Therefore, it's mandatory that the child do well.

Parents who count on their children to furnish a sense of self-worth may stand out in a crowd . . . at a ball game, for instance, where a mother screams exhortations to her child from the sidelines, then jeers when the child falls short. They may also appear in a subtler guise—the fellow at work who lists his kids' achievements at the drop of a hat, the mother who can always top any mention of your child's activities with rave notices about her own. Whatever form it takes, whenever the child is involved, the parent acts as though it's his or her fate in the balance, his or her accomplishments being judged. In a sense, it is.

It's not difficult to see how unwelcome or even dangerous an angry child seems to such a parent. Through the parent's distorted lens, the angry child appears unhappy. And an unhappy child represents failure . . . again. The parent's already shaky self-esteem plummets farther. It's also likely, in these situations, that the parent identifies with the angry and helpless child, leaping to the conclusion that the child's unhappiness is serious and long-term, like the parent's. All this can be set in motion simply because a child gets mad, a normal occurrence in everyday life.

## Personality Traits That Give Rise to Problems with Angry Children

*Dependency.* Usually frightened and rather desperate, the dependent person places a premium on maintaining relationships in order not to be alone. Achieving this means cultivating characteristics that will ensure the good opinion of others. Anger, of course, isn't one of the characteristics. Dependent people believe that angry feelings will lead to alienation and rejection, which is disastrous, if one is bent upon being agreeable. Someone who's governed by dependency finds anger frightening and comes to abhor it, along with any sort of conflict and friction.

*Egocentricity.* Especially common among people we call narcissists, egocentric people strive for admiration at all costs. They are quite dependent upon others, of course, but in a quite different way from the dependent sort described above. Egocentric types aren't necessarily eager to be liked and accepted. They need to be the object of awe and admiration. Angry children threaten them because anger insults their pride and because it makes them suspect that they've failed to convince others—even children—of their incredible abilities.

*Martyrdom.* A person who is a martyr suffers endlessly in the service of higher goals. The martyr is always rising above something, putting aside personal needs, sacrificing for the greater good, and hoping to be rewarded with gratitude. Appreciation and thanks are necessary to the martyr, and there's no way the behavior of an angry child can be construed as such. Upsets can cause great personal misery in the martyr. The child who has provoked the upset is often made to feel guilty; the martyr is a master at inducing guilt. It is how he or she gets even with the angry child who has disturbed the equilibrium and peace of the family.

*Revengefulness.* The revengeful person seeks compliance with his or her wishes no matter what anyone else feels, wants, or thinks. Anger, especially in a child, is akin to mutiny and the revengeful type doesn't find it difficult to rationalize acting vindictively to stamp it out. Because of their lack of regard for others' rights and their lack of remorse when they violate them, it can be dangerous to express anger with such people.

*Knowing everything.* Because there's room for only one opinion on virtually any subject, such a person has little tolerance for anger from anyone. When it's a child who's mad, the know-it-all is likely to be roused to searing and contemptuous criticism. Sometimes, the mere expression of an opinion of any sort from a child—not even an angry one—may provoke this response.

Every reader probably sees some aspects of himself or herself in this chapter, and that's positive. Awareness of attitudes or personality characteristics that may predispose us to mishandle a child's anger will immediately diminish our likelihood of doing so. Self-diagnosis can be followed by self-help. Once sensitive to our own difficulties with anger, we can make deliberate efforts to curtail them.

## CONCEPTS TO REMEMBER TO PREVENT MISHANDLING ANGER

• Try not to repeat the past. It is a good idea to look back on our own pasts and examine how angry feelings were handled in our homes. As we progress as parents and caretakers, we will come over and over again to the same issues our parents confronted when raising us. Now that we are older, we can evaluate the constructiveness of our own parents' attitudes. We don't necessarily have to repeat the past if we know better.

• Anger is still a highly conflictual and hotly debated issue in society today, which causes a lot of confusion. Fanatical and extreme attitudes toward this feeling come from people who do not see anger as a natural feeling. These attitudes may be held by experts as well. Thus, it is understandable that many of us are confused. To lessen this confusion, it is good to remember that anger is like all other natural feelings, and in our children, it is as whole-some as any other.

- A child is rarely spoiled from having her normal needs, often communicated by anger, gratified in an age-appropriate manner. You need not fear ca-pitulating in order to fill your child's natural needs. A "spoiled child" is one who has learned that anger isn't okay or useful, and has started to use anger to manipulate caretakers, who are either fright-ened of this feeling or who secretly feel the same way.

- Control is an essential aspect of proper child rear-ing. Many things need to be controlled, such as the safety of the environment, the amount of stimula-tion, the degree of stress to which a child is ex-posed, and the type and degree of certain behaviors of a child so as to ward off destructive-ness. When our need for control is excessive, the problems begin. To know when we err in this di-rection, it is good to ask ourselves the following questions:

Is my need for control based on objective knowl-edge or simply based on my own driven need to have it my way?

Do I have knowledge of something bad happening if my way isn't followed, or do I just imagine it happening?

Is my child really able to control herself in the way that I demand?

Am I generally an overly controlled person in at least several areas?

- Many of us carry around excess "emotional baggage," and we might over- or underreact when confronted with a normally angry child, one with whom we overidentify. If we find ourselves doing this, there's a good chance that we are reacting to our own pasts. At this point, we have to begin working on resolving these past problems so that we can see clearly in the present. Self-examination is the first step toward achieving this end.

- Changing our personality is difficult but possible. The main ingredient for such change is motivation, which takes an honest appraisal of oneself. As difficult as this may be, the rewards in terms of personal happiness and the welfare of one's children make up for this many times over. This exploration of why we mishandle anger, if done with compassion and honesty, can only serve to decrease the chances of our passing on our own difficulties in this area.

# CHAPTER THREE

# How We Mishandle Children's Anger

All adults have some trouble handling children's anger. As we have seen, some of us have a lot of difficulty in this area because we bring one or more of the characteristics described in Chapter Two to our interactions with our children. Whatever the trouble may be, it boils down to the same thing. The adult perceives the child's angry feelings as a threat. When we feel threatened, we try to defend ourselves. Anger in our children, unfortunately, becomes a feeling that must be dealt with defensively—the beginning of the mishandling of anger.

We've all heard and probably even used the term "defense mechanism," the human psyche's way of protecting itself against something that it registers as dangerous. When an angry child is perceived by a parent as dangerous or threatening, this parent automatically mobilizes his or her psychological defense mechanisms in order to ward off the resulting anxiety that comes with a threat. In such situations, these parents' inner defense mechanisms are converted into what might be called "offense mechanisms." Parents use these offense mechanisms to block their own awareness of their child's anger, and in some cases they try to extinguish any trace of anger altogether. As the saying goes, a good offense is often the best defense, and when it comes to angry children, parents frequently agree.

Parents may try a direct assault on the offending anger—meting out punishment when a child gets mad, for example—or indirect maneuvers, such as bribing the child. The goal, however, is the same: to do away with the child's angry feelings.

Trying to rob a child of a natural feeling, to stifle his emotional expression, is bad enough in itself. Unfortunately, offense mechanisms are often compounded by accompanying rationalizations. When we're dealing with kids, we adults are experts at concocting elaborate reasons for our behavior and, of course, we can argue more effectively than our children since we've had more experience. All too often, as we mishandle our children's anger, we also offer seemingly plausible and rational reasons for doing so. We convince ourselves and our children that we're right.

The following is a general survey of some of the most common offense mechanisms, or tactics, that adults use to abolish children's anger. Some of these I've observed in my practice, some in daily life. Of course, the list isn't complete. Adults, I'm sorry to say, are endlessly inventive when it comes to ducking children's anger, and certainly there are many variations on the following general themes.

You will probably see yourself in this section, as well. We all mishandle anger sometimes. What is important to remember is that the chronic and repetitive mishandling of children's anger does the most harm over time.

## DIRECT OFFENSE MECHANISMS

### Anger Denial

Any list of defense mechanisms will include denial. Denial is generally defined as a primarily unconscious and automatic means of refusing to acknowledge something. Alcoholics, for example, are said to be in denial when they continually fail to see that they have a problem with drinking. Denial, in effect, renders someone emotionally blind. Whatever he's trying to avoid doesn't exist to him.

If this common defense has been turned into an offense mechanism against a child's anger, the parent won't see the anger; it won't even enter his awareness. Should the situation be brought to the parent's attention, he'll most likely greet the news with disbelief and dismissal of the messenger. The label "crazy-making" is a good way to describe an environment that's governed by denial. A sense of unreality permeates everything.

Some years ago, a father concerned about his ten-year-old son's persistent school failure came to see me. The father noted that his son was pale, listless, depressed, hunched over, and didn't look well. It mattered a great deal to the father that his son perform well at school. He felt that the "superior education" he and his own father got at this school was crucial to their success.

As the father outlined the problem and traced its history, it became clear that the difficulties began when his son was forced to transfer to this new school in the third grade. Obvious signs of anger then appeared. At first, the boy protested directly, loudly, and angrily; he didn't want to make the move and leave his old friends. His protests ignored, he then began dawdling around the house in the morning, finding reasons not to leave for school. His behavior at home became increasingly belligerent. Eventually, he refused to go away to camp during the summer. Now he was failing in school.

When I saw the boy, his smoldering rage was obvious. His father had forced him to leave a school and group of friends that he liked in favor of a school he disliked and one that, in fact, left him feeling out of his depth due to various learning difficulties. Most aggravating of all, however, was that his father was unable to understand how angry his son was. When the son and I, together, finally confronted the father with this anger, he simply smiled at us as if we were a bit nutty. Our

*further efforts in this direction were never any
more successful than the first one. The man would
not and could not permit himself to see his child
as angry. He continued instead to focus on what
I might do to help the boy "buckle down" at school.
I know how exasperated I became with this situation, so imagine how the son must have felt.*

*The good news—and the bad news—is that
eventually the boy was expelled from the school.
This allowed him to go to a school with less rig-
orous standards and an atmosphere in which he
could flourish with much less anger. For a long
time afterward, however, it also left him feeling
as though he were stupid.*

Mishandling a child's anger with denial produces
a sterile atmosphere in a household. It stops the normal ebb and flow of human relations. When we live
with others, everyday events inevitably produce at
least fleeting frustrations. Imagine living in a situation where this wasn't understood and where anger
was met by no response at all. It must feel like being
in a strange neighborhood, asking directions, and receiving a blank stare in return. People who deny anger speak a different emotional language from
people who don't—and it's extremely difficult for angry children to be heard and understood.

## Anger Neglect

Anger neglect is closely related to denial in that it also tries to eliminate the perception of anger. Rather than refusing to acknowledge a child's anger, however, the neglecting parent registers the anger but adopts the attitude that if she doesn't pay attention to it, maybe it will go away. Although somewhat less buried than denial, neglect still has the same malignant effect on a child: the anger remains unheard.

*This strategy was certainly operating one day as I sat in a clinic with the mother of four-year-old Harry and his two-year-old sister, Anne. The screams coming from where they were playing indicated that the two were at odds over sharing Harry's new game, but when their mother and I looked over, things were momentarily calm. When the shrieks resumed, though, the mother continued to seem unfazed. She'd recently read a book, she told me, that said siblings often argued and that this wasn't a problem. Letting them work things out themselves was, in fact, good training for experiences they'd encounter as they grew up. The principle was sound, but I still had my reservations, based on the children's ages and the nature of their howls. After awhile, Harry came over to us, his eyelid bleeding from a cut his sister had inflicted with one of the plastic game pieces. Some education about child development, sibling relations, and general safety followed in short order.*

*I'd been treating Elaine for depression for about three months when she told me that her daughter had been misbehaving in school. Apparently, she frequently became angry with other children when she had to share materials or the teacher's attention. Because this was uncharacteristic behavior for the daughter, and I knew that it could be related to her mother's depression, I asked to see her. She was an utterly delightful girl—effervescent, creative, engaging—and a distinct contrast to her mother. Since becoming depressed, the mother was lethargic, pessimistic, and rather forbidding. Also, because her depression made her constantly tired, she'd lost her ability to really respond to her daughter as she had in the past. Every few hours she took a nap, and when she woke up, her daughter was often needy and angry. The mother simply didn't have the energy to do anything about it. She just hoped the anger would go away.*

In this instance, the mother's consistent neglect of her daughter's everyday anger signals led the child to act out in school. When the mother recovered, her daughter's anger completely disappeared.

## Anger Eradication

Unfortunately, some parents probably spend more time and energy trying to directly eradicate children's anger than they do on many other child rearing activities put together. The effect of doing this is just as abnormal and stunting as trying to wipe out a child's hunger—anger is as vital a part of the human organism.

A trip I took to a shopping mall served as a mini-laboratory on the subject of anger eradication. The following events occurred within approximately two minutes:

> *In the parking lot, the mother of a toddler sucking on a lollipop stick told him to stop because he could choke on the flimsy piece of cardboard—a point well taken. When the toddler refused and began wailing, his mother tried to wrench the stick out of his mouth and simultaneously haul him out of his car seat. While he wrestled against her, she yelled. By the time she got the stick away and the child free of the seat, she was so aggravated that she began shaking the child, hollering at him to listen, to understand what she was saying, and to stop acting up.*

It would have been more effective had the mother calmly and firmly taken the lollipop before trying to move the child.

*A school-age child walking with his father asked if he could buy a videotape. When the father said no, and the youngster muttered a four-letter expletive, the father ordered him to return to the hot car while the father went on to do his shopping. The boy had a chance to use the expletive again as he headed back toward the car.*

An explanation of reasons, rather than a flat no, might have lessened the boy's anger, and possibly a warning about profane language might have kept the situation from escalating.

*Entering a store, I saw a family of five, the children aged roughly two to seven, posing for a fledgling photographer. While he fiddled with his equipment, the kids were told to hold the pose. I'm sure their idea of fun and games at the mall wasn't standing still for a photograph. Each time they began to fidget, the mother grabbed their arms and, finally, the father began yelling at them not to move. The children, of course, just got angrier the more the parents clamped down.*

As in the last example, the parents might have done better to remind the kids what fun they'd be having shortly, instead of focusing on their misbehavior.

The effort to eradicate anger may take many forms. Sometimes it's a nasty look that conveys disgust or a warning of future punishment. Other times it's simply a pointed finger. Lectures might be one parent's style, while another favors action, such as removing a child from a social situation. Then there are the unmistakable, overt strategies designed to quash anger outright: punishment, criticism, and humiliation.

Parents who need to use these tactics to eradicate anger in their children have generally been given a poor anger education themselves. They have little tolerance for what they feel anger represents. Generally, these beliefs grow from a given context, such as a set of religious premises or a particular value system or certain cultural notions the parents were brought up with. This context furnishes the parents with ready-made rationalizations for their behavior such as that anger is the devil's handiwork, it's for the child's own good, or certain realities must be understood in order to function in the world.

Paradoxically, these people are quick to become angry themselves—an inheritance from their childhoods in which they were on the receiving end of the very anger eradication measures they're now using on their own children. They never got any relief for their youthful feelings of helplessness, and they may have hair-trigger tempers as a result.

This, of course, only deepens their children's confusion. The parent is likely to fly off the handle at any time, but he tells the child that she mustn't do the same. The child knows this is unfair; she recognizes the double standard, but there's nowhere for her to turn for recourse. Parents who operate this way place little value on discussion or on exploring a child's feelings. In fact, they probably see such endeavors as a waste of time.

Parents who are attempting to stamp out anger in their children frequently humiliate them in front of others. Of course this embarrasses the child and onlookers as well.

*Not long ago at a picnic, I watched a father talking about business with his partner while his nine-year-old son continually interrupted, trying to get his dad's attention. At first, the father simply shot sharp glances in his son's direction, but as the child's insistence became louder, angrier, and more pointed, the sound level of the father's response rose also. Finally, the father began yelling insults at his son, telling him he was no better than a wild animal, that he didn't know how to behave, that he had no manners.*

The father's disgust and disappointment was obvious, to say the least; his son ran off crying, without the father ever knowing what had been bothering the boy in the first place. Interrupting someone may be rude, but should that have been the overriding concern here? There were many ways the father might have handled this situation without resorting to overkill. He could have listened in the first place, or at least tuned in when he noticed his child's anger. The best choice would have been to take a short time out from his conversation to focus on his son's needs. The choice he made was utterly unproductive and one of the most damaging for his child.

## INDIRECT OFFENSE MECHANISMS

The direct mechanisms used in mishandling anger that I've dealt with so far—denial, neglect, and overt eradication—all try to stifle the expression of anger. There are other types of mishandling that, superficially may appear to allow and even encourage the expression of angry feelings. The aim of these offense mechanisms, however, is the same: to do away with the child's anger and to minimize its impact on the adult. Because these strategies are indirect and not always obvious, they carry with them an additional element of confusion.

### Oversoothing Anger

This kind of mishandling involves oversympathizing with the angry child in order to decrease angry feelings. Immediate and engulfing sympathy from a parent robs the child of the experience of revealing fully and/or discovering the original cause of the anger. It has the quality of a preemptive strike in that it prevents the anger from really getting off the ground. It's hard for a child to rant, cry, argue, withdraw—or express anger in whatever way is characteristic of him—when he's awash in a wave of comfort and commiseration. This overwhelming so-licitousness, in effect, shuts him up.

Some adults who use this strategy haven't learned to handle anger themselves. Openly angry displays may frighten them. They can become panicky when they sense that anger may be just around the corner, before it's even visible or audible.

Soothing away anger also spoils a child, but not in the way that we usually use that phrase. Again, what gets spoiled is the child's chance to learn that anger is a normal, healthy feeling that can elicit a helpful response and result in diminished distress. This les-son gets short-circuited when a parent mishandles anger by leaping in with smothering sympathy. The child never comes to know that anger is transient, that it can be tolerated without immediate assis-tance, and that one can develop inner resources to cope with it.

When a child is deprived of this knowledge be-cause her parent is always on guard against her ex-periencing anger, she comes to believe that angry feelings are potentially catastrophic, an attitude that's probably close to her parent's. This isn't the only problem that oversoothing will leave her with. She'll also tend to have greater than usual anxiety about simple interactions in life, because now she'll be on guard against any anger getting through the internal barriers she's set up. Of course, she'll also be stuck with the original anger.

*A nineteen-year-old woman was brought to me after she'd suffered what was described as a "breakdown." According to her parents, this college student had become unable to concentrate or to sleep, had gone into a deep depression accompanied by endless crying, had experienced decreased appetite and fatigue, and was expressing suicidal ideas. Because the young woman had trouble describing her present problems when she was alone with me, I asked her mother to join us. The moment she came in, she immediately asked her daughter how she was, lit a cigarette for her, and pushed a box of tissues in her direction. The daughter seemed disconcerted by her mother's behavior, but she also accepted it, however grudgingly.*

*The mother began by describing the despair she felt over her daughter's condition. She understood why the rejection her daughter had received from a sorority had catapulted her into a depression. What other response could she have had? But time would take care of it, she reassured her daughter; there were other sororities who'd be happy to have her.*

Over time, as I got to know this family, I recognized that the mother's behavior that first day was the tip of the iceberg in the over-soothing department. Throughout her daughter's life, anticipating every bump in the developmental road, the mother had tried to engineer the complete avoidance of helplessness and anger for her child, ostensibly to spare her the pain inherent in growing up. The result, of course, was that she had utterly stifled her daughter and kept her from developing any coping skills of her own. The present circumstances, a quite ordinary social setback with some accompanying anger, had caused the girl to panic and feel she was coming unglued, because she'd never dealt with any difficulty on her own. Also, in this case, the link between soothing away anger and overprotectiveness was evident. Both of these approaches invariably mask hidden agendas of the parents; and both also have the effect of dwarfing the child's development of a full self that's able to roll with life's punches.

## Compliance

Compliance appears to be the exact opposite of anger eradication. Here, the parent is the one who seems forced to toe the line, to be pushed around by the child. It appears as though a role reversal has taken place: The child calls the shots, and the parent is the target of caustic remarks and bullying behavior. I've been astonished by families that operate this way, with the children carping about everything from food to vacation choices, dictating the course of such things as medical care and home purchases, and the parents going along with it all.

The dynamic that often operates when the parent-child relationship is stood on its head in this way is that the parents, still very much in the grip of the anger they feel toward their own parents, invest everything in pleasing their kids. They hope, by doing so, to prevent their children from feeling the kind of anger they've been carrying around all their lives. This isn't any more effective than all the other ways of mishandling anger, and it only ends up damaging the child in ways the parents don't foresee.

## Bribes

This common offense consists of the parent offering something special to the child in exchange for his abandoning angry feelings. Parents who employ this strategy fear anger so much that they try, in effect, to buy it out of existence. Here's how the transaction goes: if you stop crying or start smiling or quiet down, I'll let you have some of the ice cream I've been saving for dessert or get you that new catcher's mitt you've been wanting or take you to the movies this weekend.

Bribery pacts are as far from healthy, constructive anger handling as one can get. Not only does the parent make no effort to find out why the child's angry, but he or she changes the focus to making the anger disappear. Not only does the anger and its cause go unaddressed, the child is taught that anger will buy treats.

This way of dealing with anger has the allure that's often attached to a quick fix. Probably many of us have occasionally found ourselves bribing away anger without meaning to make it a habit. We all know how it feels to have an angry child standing before us at exactly the moment when we feel we can't possibly deal with the situation: a youngster is throwing a tantrum and dinner guests are due in five minutes; we've just taken an important phone call and our teenager insists on launching into a lecture about his civil rights and how they apply to using the car that night; we're sharing a private moment with our mate when an enraged child bursts into the bedroom.

The bribe, a convenient stopgap, may be tempting, but over the long haul, bribing away a child's anger is very damaging. And once set up, the expectation that anger will lead to special treatment dies hard. Kids can learn very quickly how to approach us at those times when we're most vulnerable to taking this seemingly easy way out.

## Refusal to Set Limits

When parents don't set limits, they let a child's anger escalate to the point at which it becomes destructive to the child or others. A parent who refuses to set limits may even stimulate a child's anger by letting it go unchecked. Parents who do this often carry about a lot of barely suppressed, unexpressed anger themselves. Their child's out-of-control anger allows them to experience their own angry feelings vicariously and unconsciously. Remember the father who claimed to be upset with his son's quarrels with friends but, in fact, seemed to relish the boy's troublemaking?

The refusal to set limits may take different forms. Perhaps the parent simply overlooks the child's anger as it escalates to tantrum proportions. Maybe she condones it without any understanding of the underlying issues; she gives blanket approval to the anger without knowing the circumstances. "You're right, Jimmy," she may tell her son. "No one should ever push you around," or "It was fine that you told off Suzie. She deserved it."

These parents may suggestively push a child toward anger by automatically defending their angry child against others whom they see as victimizers. Often feeling like losers themselves, such parents are quite competitive and, through their children, they have a chance to win. They may resent limits themselves and harbor all sorts of rebellious tendencies. The child, of course—stimulated to pursue destructive ends—gets sacrificed in the process.

Exploring the various strategies that parents use to mishandle children's anger makes clear that not only does mishandling prevent a healthy exchange between parent and child in the present, it also sows the seeds of future difficulty for the child. When a parent continually responds to a child's anger in one of the ways I've described, it necessarily adds to the child's sense of frustration and helplessness, because she doesn't get help with the problem that made her angry in the first place. Her distress goes unrelieved. She learns, by example, some erroneous lessons about anger. All these factors combine to influence the child to begin to treat her own angry feelings in destructive ways. That is the beginning of the process of the anger metamorphosis, and its results are a host of serious psychological difficulties: the legacies of mishandled anger.

## STEPS TO AVOID MISHANDLING ANGER

- Survey your behaviors for a few days to see if, in fact, you perceive anger as a threat that makes you anxious. How do you handle this?
- Do you never see your child as angry? If so, then odds are that you are in denial. You should be certain to read on in this book to familiarize yourself with the various forms of anger in children and then apply this knowledge to your child.
- Do you avoid anger in your child by neglect or with one of the indirect mechanisms mentioned above? If so, odds are you shy away from confrontations in general. This needs attention not only for your child's anger management but for all the areas of your own life that could benefit from assertion. You could start with little steps at home such as discussing anger in the family or expressing your own anger more. You could also concentrate on asserting your own needs in many everyday situations. Finally, you could go to any of the many self-assertion programs that focus on overcoming inhibitions and learning constructive expressions of feelings.

- Are you an anger eradicator? Do you meet all anger with your own? If so, odds are that you have had a poor anger education. For you, a detailed reading of the chapters on causes of anger in children as well as constructive handling of anger is essential.
- Finally, if you feel you are prone to child abuse you must get professional help now. Please read the following special section on child abuse and then Chapter Nine, which gives advice on seeking professional help for anger problems.

## CHILD ABUSE—A SPECIAL FORM OF ANGER ERADICATION

Sometimes anger eradication measures may cross the line into excessive physical punishment and child abuse. In such instances, a child's angry message not only goes unheard, but the messenger becomes the target.

Child abuse has received increasingly intense publicity as we've become more aware of how widespread it is. Unfortunately, we'd have to double the number of cases reported even to come close to a true picture of how often this abuse occurs.

It seems obvious that people who inflict physical harm on their children have great trouble with anger, but sometimes the obvious needs restating. I think of the woman who told me in all seriousness that her husband wasn't angry when he regularly beat their child. "He's always calm when he does it," she said.

"He never gets mad. It's just part of trying to teach our daughter a lesson." I guess this falls into the for-her-own-good school of punishment, which is often the rationalization for obvious child abuse. It also illustrates that someone needn't be tearing his hair out, screaming and yelling, breaking up the house, and generally acting like a wild man, in order to have severe anger problems.

Adults have varying levels of tolerance for helplessness, just as children do. Child abusers have little tolerance for such feelings in themselves and in their children. Grown-ups who physically harm children are quick to anger, and their anger is intense. They can't bear to feel powerless and out of control for any length of time, and it doesn't take much for them to reach their frustration threshold. When they're inundated by feelings of helplessness, they respond with violence that may take the form of beatings with fists, burnings (with cigarettes, hot irons, or scalding water), choking, hitting with straps or other such improvised weapons as electric wires, pieces of wood, exercise bars, or anything else that's within reach. Any such violence can cause serious injuries and is potentially fatal.

Parents who abuse their children had their own anger mishandled as they were growing up and nearly always were abused themselves. Usually, their anger educations consisted of little more than learning that when they expressed anger, it was met by violence. They carry within them great stores of counter-hostility or the tendency to meet anger with anger. They often feel to blame for the abuse that happened to them as children. Consequently, they feel guilty and have poor self-images. They commonly feel unworthy, ashamed, and even loathsome.

Try though they might to shake the feeling, they identify with or feel similar to both the abusive parent as well as the bad, victimized child. They're stuck in this bind, a set-up for disaster. To further complicate their conflicts, they frequently hope to discover in their own children someone who will treat them the way they ought to have been treated when they were children: with loving attention and concern. When they're met instead by a child who requires parenting from them and is often just showing normal angry feelings, their lifelong frustration and rage grows even greater.

For child abuse to occur, though, it takes more than just an angry child or a history of abuse. Usually, a number of chronic stresses are present as well, such as financial difficulties, illness, a sense of isolation, marital problems and, especially, substance abuse.

The following components commonly set the stage for child abuse: a high-risk parent, a stress-laden environment, and a child who is perceived as expressing anger. Add to this an increase in stress or a bout of intoxication, and we have all the elements for catastrophe.

There are other factors that are associated with child abuse as well, and these can help predict potential abuse and can prevent abuse from happening to another child:

- Does the parent have a history of violent behavior outside the home, or is the parent extremely volatile emotionally? Does he tend, for example, to have altercations that end up in fistfights? Does he have the proverbial short fuse when it comes to anger, or does he have extreme mood swings?
- Is the parent impulsive and given to activities that go with that trait, such as gambling or stealing?
- Is the parent depressed? Someone who's mired in a long-term bad mood is bound to feel a fair amount of irritation and frustration. Often, with such a person, a seemingly minor annoyance can be the straw that breaks the camel's back, the trigger for abuse. Histories of depression often precede acts of violence, and they should always be warning signals of potential abuse. This is especially true if the person who is depressed has a tendency toward violence.
- Does the parent abuse alcohol or other substances? We know that violent behavior often occurs when people are under the influence of chemical substances, especially alcohol. The most common drug in our society, alcohol is known to loosen inner restraints and release us from inhibitions and prohibitions.
- Is this a single parent family? Abuse is statistically more common in these situations, and one can understand why this is the case. Raising children is a

large and demanding job. Doing it alone can increase the stress in a parent's life.

### Am I Committing Child Abuse?

Many parents ask if they might be committing child abuse when they flare up irrationally, lose their tempers, impose an unnecessarily harsh punishment, or even verbally assault a child vindictively. All of these actions are potentially abusive if they occur with any regularity. It's not always easy to draw a precise line between a parent's expression of anger and abuse. Life itself is never that clear.

When parents are on rare occasions unduly severe or even cruel, if they realize how harmful this treatment is, quickly get control of themselves, and talk to the child about the situation, they're not committing child abuse in the popular sense of the term. Chances are that even moments like these—if they're uncharacteristic—won't leave scars.

*One mother I recall had just had her bathroom painted when her curious two-year-old got hold of a bottle of nail polish, attempted to open it, and spattered bright red streaks across one pristine wall. In the heat of the moment, she hurled profanity and a tissue box at him—most unusual actions for her, ones she never repeated, and ones that she immediately wished she could take back.*

This one-time event didn't poison the mother-son relationship forever or set in motion a train of destructive events. It could happen to many of us.

## Is There Any Place for Physical Punishment?

Is physical punishment—rarely, sometimes, or regularly—a legitimate measure for parents to use? I believe that physical punishment damages parent-child relations and that, once begun, generally tends to increase. It's all too easy to cause physical harm when hitting a child, particularly if we're in the grip of powerful emotions, some of which we may not even understand. I'm not saying that an impulsive spank on the rear end will cause irretrievable harm, but the best rule is: Never hit a child.

Equally important is the fact that nothing good comes from physical punishment. It teaches nothing about healthy communication, about the value of talking through a situation with a child, or about how to handle one's anger constructively. It is, in fact, an object lesson in poor anger management. No one—parent or child—benefits from it. Anger, properly received and responded to, can enhance the bond between parent and child. Hitting a child can only weaken that crucial bond.

## Warning Signals of Child Abuse

Most parents who are prone to violence recognize this tendency in themselves because of their histories. Others who've never committed abuse or done anything violent sometimes are concerned that they might. If you are worried about yourself or someone you know, pay close attention to the following warning signals:

- An increase in the number and violent nature of temper tantrums may lead to abuse. Maybe you used to blow your stack once in a rare while, but now you seem to be exploding regularly. Perhaps you used to holler when you got mad, but now sometimes you throw things or slam your fist into inanimate objects.
- Developing an ongoing dislike for a particular child is especially dangerous if it gradually takes on the qualities of an obsession. Perhaps you begin to fantasize about violent acts against the child, and along with the fantasies come increasing feelings of rage. Interestingly, parents who feel this way often see a lot of themselves in the child they think of treating violently, especially those qualities of their own they like least.
- Parents whose anger is slipping beyond their control often feel frightened and ashamed. This causes them to put even more distance between themselves and others. Their isolation grows and their chances of getting help decrease.

Any parent who's experiencing these warning signals needs to get help immediately, before any violence occurs.

It's not easy to reach out from a position of fear and shame, but it's crucial to try to let someone know how you feel. Tell your doctor; go to a hospital emergency room; ask a friend to help arrange for professional intervention; call your local child abuse hot line. Do anything to break through the barrier of isolation around you. No matter how difficult that may seem, feelings of shame and fear will only worsen if you harm your child.

By the same token, if you know of a high-risk parent or a child who might be in danger, do whatever you can to see that they get help. We all have this responsibility and perhaps, if we all exercise it, we can begin to reverse the tragic statistics of child abuse.

## Nonphysical Abuse

Abuse that isn't physical can also hurt and damage a child. Humiliation, as I've already noted, is one of these emotionally abusive strategies used to eradicate anger. Some others are treating a child's anger with derision, making fun of the anger, or criticizing it in various ways. Sarcastic remarks and mimicking a child in a contemptuous way are common examples, as are flat-out rageful tirades that are intended to destroy a child's angry feelings through intimidation. These ways of attempting to directly eradicate a youngster's anger can leave scars equal to those of physical beatings.

# PART TWO

# Understanding Children

PART TWO

Understanding
Children

# CHAPTER FOUR

# What Makes Kids Angry and How They Show It

The first step in the constructive handling of anger in our children is an understanding of its causes and a familiarity with its expression. Before turning to a detailed examination of those topics, I think it is good idea to understand how anger is shaped in each of our children.

*Whenever six-year-old Molly was going to speak, she wanted everyone to stop what they were doing and pay rapt attention. With three siblings and busy professional parents, it was understandable that she felt that her turn might come and go rather quickly, if it came at all. When told she'd have to wait her turn, however, she'd protest loudly. If not given the floor immediately, she'd yell in a prolonged monotone that drowned out anyone else in the room.*

*Seven-year-old Charlie often burst into his parents bedroom unannounced, always with an ur-*

*gent issue: He needed help with his homework; something had to be fixed immediately; his brothers were picking on him. His parents—whether sleeping, resting, or otherwise occupied—generally took a few moments to gather themselves before considering Charlie's complaint. His response was to begin whimpering, his eyes filling with tears, then head off to his room, seeming injured beyond repair.*

*Jennie, a shy girl, felt severely strained by the increased social activities that came with adolescence. One day she dragged in from school, monosyllabic and morose. Only after she'd received a call from a friend did she let her parents know that she'd been hurt and enraged by being rejected for membership in a high school sorority.*

Each child has a special style of anger expression, such as high-decibel outbursts, silent withdrawal, or logical argument. This is determined, to a large extent, by what I call "anger shapers." These shapers include:

- The child's stress tolerance
- Age
- Gender
- Temperament
- Role models including those in the family as well as those in the culture

## STRESS TOLERANCE

Anyone who has observed children carefully knows that what enrages one may leave another unfazed. There are complicated reasons for these differences, but perhaps the most important is stress tolerance, a child's ability to withstand feelings of discomfort, pain, environmental tension, and frustration. To some degree, this individual tolerance is an inborn, biological trait that shows up in the earliest days of life. Just think of a nursery full of newborns: a wide variety of capacities to tolerate discomfort of various sorts will be on display. What frustrates one infant, will be accepted placidly by another.

Parents almost invariably comment on how different one child in the family is from another, right from the beginning. The difference the parents often focus on is how each child responds to stresses that cause helplessness and accompanying anger.

*In a recent consultation with Rich's parents, they described their teenager's increasingly aggressive, negative attitude toward the family. He ignored everything they said, was performing poorly and behaving defiantly in school, and met any attempts at help with intimidation. With Rich about to be expelled, they decided to seek help.*

*I discovered that their son's behavior had ac-*

*tually been going on for years. The parents had simply managed, until now, to keep it under control by giving in to Rich's demands, transferring him to a new school when things got out of hand, and drinking heavily each night to blot out their own feelings of helplessness about the situation.*

*When I inquired about their other child, they quickly told me what a dream he was compared to Rich, how wonderful he'd been from the time he was born: calm, easy to please, seldom expressing discomfort. Rich, on the other hand, had always been troublesome: fussy as an infant, aggressive with other children from the time he was a toddler, and a problem in school from day one.*

Obviously, these two boys had very different capacities to tolerate stress. Whether or not we see these differences as dictated by biology, by the environment or, as is more likely, by a combination of the two, they illustrate an important point: Each child has a unique stress tolerance. Ideally, we all want to tailor our child rearing practices to a particular child, making allowances for differences, treating each as an individual. A child's stress tolerance, which shapes her overall anger profile, is an important guide in that regard.

## AGE

A child's age, of course, also has great bearing on anger expression. The younger a child is the more diffuse this expression will be. The physical display of an infant's angry feelings—crying, red-faced, arms and legs thrashing—is worlds away from the sophisticated lecture meted out by an angry teenager, for instance. As children grow and their skills increase, they develop different ways of expressing themselves. In general, when it comes to anger, these forms of expression change from the global and physical to more pointed and specific mental and verbal means.

## GENDER

In addition to stress tolerance and age, gender is also an anger-shaper. Most people assume that boys are more aggressive than girls and may conclude from this that boys experience more anger. This isn't the case, but I think our culture does condition boys to express anger more openly than girls, or in more obvious ways. Imprisoned by stereotypes that say boys are rougher or more active, girls more delicate and passive, parents and other adults may be more likely to tolerate a particular kind of angry display in a son—a physical acting out, let's say—than they would in a daughter.

This doesn't mean that girls feel any less anger than boys, or that they don't express it. In fact, in the earliest years, it's been my experience—and that of other professionals—that girls are more given to openly angry displays. Perhaps this occurs before the full effects of cultural expectations take over. Once they do, it's likely—though not always the case—that girls' expressions of anger will become somewhat less obvious and more disguised.

*I recently watched a neighborhood softball game my children were involved in. When a boy came off the field after missing an easy pop-up, he kicked the bench, cursing a blue streak, and tossed down his glove. On the other hand, when a girl on the opposing team struck out with two on base, her shoulders slumped and she walked back to the bench, looking as though she wished she were invisible.*

## TEMPERAMENT

Another anger-shaper is the innate, unique combination of characteristics we call temperament, or disposition. In addition to stress tolerance, our activity levels, sensitivities, general mood variability, degree of energy, and ways of bonding are just some of the things at least partially determined by our biological heritage. All of these go into molding our temperaments, and they affect how we show anger.

Of course, some of these characteristics are also colored by the way we're raised. Haven't a great many of us heard at one time or another in our lives—starting when we were children—that we were "sensitive" or "hot-headed" or "sunny" or "impatient" or some other adjective that was meant to describe our basic take on life? As limited—and perhaps self-fulfilling—as these labels might be, they probably do indicate something about our basic natures, and these labels play a part in how we all express angry feelings: intensely, mildly, instantly, rarely, openly, furtively. This is true for children, too.

## ROLE MODELS

Role modeling—what kids see around them—is the final anger-shaper, and it has a decisive effect on a child's anger expression. This modeling comes from a combination of the family anger atmosphere, as well as from the culture at large.

The family anger atmosphere is created by a combination of things: parental attitudes toward anger, the relationship between the parents and how anger is expressed, and parental tolerance for conflict, to name a few. Children learn quickly what's acceptable and what isn't, whether anger is rewarded or punished. Generally, they will adopt the style of emotional expression they observe in their parents.

As mentioned earlier, some families seem fueled by the constant and ear-splitting expression of anger.

Other families may tolerate no raised voices at all, and insist on polite, sensible discussion. Still others may have an atmosphere of virtual silence and palpable tension. Whatever the habitual family tone, it will influence how kids express their anger.

Children, of course, are exposed to the culture. At first, this is mostly through their parents, as representatives of this culture. As they grow older, there is less of a parental go-between, and the culture affects many of their ideas more directly, including the expression of anger. Our late twentieth-century culture imparts information impersonally, graphically, and at high speeds. Through marvels of creative engineering, children can receive enormous amounts of detailed information in a relatively short period of time. They are awash in cultural messages and images that make lasting impressions on them, and many of these concern anger.

Think of some of the things that our children witness in their living rooms or neighborhood movie theaters alone: war, acts of personal violence (including rape, murder, and hostage-taking), nuclear threats, and the poverty-induced erosion of populations. To a large degree children learn by internalizing what they perceive. This exposure cannot help but mold the minds of many of our children and sanction the huge upsurge in the impulsive, explosive, and violent explosion in anger expression.

Something that always brings home to me how the cultural atmosphere has changed since I was growing up is the miming of gunplay, whether it is a game of war, cowboys and Indians, cops and robbers, or perhaps a more current version of those old stand-bys. In my generation, we aped the use of guns—a common pistol or rifle—that fired a single bullet: "POW! You're dead." Today, I never hear children simulating anything but the sound of an automatic weapon, mowing down a huge group of people all at once.

Keeping in mind that each of our children is unique in her particular anger-shaping experiences, let's turn to examining the universal causes and expressions of anger in children of different ages.

## THE MOST COMMON EXPRESSIONS OF ANGER IN CHILDREN AND THEIR CAUSES

The first step in learning how to handle anger is to familiarize ourselves with its most common causes and expressions. In general, anger inducers fall into two general categories.

*Developmental anger* is associated with predictable causes that children encounter during the natural course of development, which are related to the frustrations encountered as milestones are approached and accomplished.

*Interpersonal anger* is generated as a result of the many different normal frustrations encountered in human relations.

Nothing to do with human personality is ever simple and tidy. These divisions aren't absolute, by any means. We all know, for example, that interpersonal relations have an effect on a child's growth and development at all ages, and vice versa. In order to understand our childrens' anger, however, I think it is a helpful distinction to make. Again please keep in mind that the angry expressions discussed here are quite natural and shouldn't be taken as indications of pathology or severe problems. They're intended simply to familiarize you with some of the ways children behave when they're mad.

As you acquaint yourself with how your particular child expresses anger, it's also important to remember that a direct cause-and-effect connection isn't always obvious. For instance, a girl who's disparaging her little brother isn't necessarily mad at him but might be frustrated about being overlooked when invitations were being given out for an important party. The youngster who helps himself to several extra packages of gum near the supermarket checkout counter probably isn't angry with the store owner. He may just have learned that he won't be in the starting lineup in the big game next weekend.

## CAUSES OF DEVELOPMENTAL ANGER
## IN INFANCY

This phase of growth, which lasts for roughly a year and a half, begins with the baby becoming used to the infinite stimuli of life outside the womb, as well as learning how to cope with ever-changing bodily feelings. While these bodily feelings change throughout childhood and adolescence, the infant has the least developed equipment to deal with them. Still undeveloped mentally, unable to filter out some sensations and to allow others, he or she is easily overwhelmed.

The primary task at this time in life is the establishment of a healthy bond with the baby's caretakers, one that will serve as the model for all future relationships as a child's life unfolds.

Make no mistake about it: infants have angry feelings. They're expressed directly, and they serve the extremely important function of communicating needs. Without them, an infant would have little chance of receiving proper care.

The younger the child, the more he or she depends upon others for help. Infants need someone else to do nearly everything for them. Being so helpless, they are vulnerable to the attitudes, wishes, and whims of those around them. They're also very sensitive to outside factors such as changes in temperature or noise level, deprivation of human contact and environmental stimuli as well as to internal shifts caused by such factors as digestive tension and mild illness. To babies, every stimulus is equally large. There is little ability to filter or discriminate various stimuli.

Helpless in the face of nearly everything and operating with immature mental faculties, an infant's distress escalates and becomes global very quickly.

When a parent sees this anger, there are several obvious places to look for its cause.

- Is the baby hungry?
- Are his clothes uncomfortable, perhaps too tight, or pinching in a particular spot?
- Is she too hot or too cold, or experiencing an upset stomach?
- Is there an overload on the stimulus front—too much noise, attention, or food?
- Is there a lack of stimulation—not being held enough, being isolated in the house, or fed mechanically?
- Is the infant in pain—a loosened diaper pin sticking tender skin—tired, feeling ill, or does he simply need to be changed?

*Jamie was invariably cranky after her midday bottle. She'd drink the six ounces happily, begin fussing within several minutes, and scream soon after that. Attempting various ways to soothe her, Jamie's mother soon discovered that two more ounces of formula did the trick. Jamie's anger indicated that for her afternoon feeding, six ounces weren't enough.*

This simple example shows how constructive and necessary anger can be. It's probably easiest for us to see anger's positive value at this most elementary stage of life. Jamie's anger tells her mother that something's wrong. Paying attention, the mother searches for the cause and finds it. Jamie's discomfort is relieved.

Something else happens as well. Jamie begins to learn trust. Establishing such a dependable, communicative human attachment in early infancy sets her on the road toward a mentally healthy life.

*John was usually docile and well-satisfied after being played with and fed, but one day, almost the moment after he was put down for his nap, he started screaming. At first, his mother was puzzled. Then she remembered that one end of the crib had been elevated earlier to help him get over a mild cold. She'd put him in the crib facing the wrong way and the blood rushing to his head was making John uncomfortable and angry.*

Infancy offers parents opportunities like this countless times each day. Our child frequently feels helpless and angry; we respond to the angry feelings and relieve the discomfort, strengthening the tie between us.

## Signs of Anger in Infancy

As noted, infants express anger in a diffuse and global way. This is because at first they can't differentiate between their minds and bodies or even between one feeling and another. Also, a very young child has little sense of how time works. He doesn't know how long an unpleasant experience will last or, in fact, that it will end at all. Easily overwhelmed by discomfort, an infant's expression of anger is complete—totally involving the mind and body—and usually nonspecific.

Take crying, for example. When an infant cries, every bit of her body is involved: lungs pour out maximum sound, nostrils flare, her skin turns red, blood pressure rises, breathing speeds up, muscles grow tense. Or kicking: both arms and legs flail furiously, even though undirected. There are no halfway measures or particular targets.

One infant may show anger by not feeding well or refusing to feed altogether. Another might display it by overzealous sucking, perhaps to the point of causing inflammation of the mother's breast. Vomiting and excessive regurgitation can be signs of anger at this stage in life, as well as colic symptoms in some cases. All of these behaviors might be caused by other reasons as well, and physical causes should be ruled out before concluding that anger is the reason.

Rest assured, if an infant is banging his head against immovable objects, he's uncomfortable and angry. Likewise with a very young child holding her breath, perhaps even until she passes out. Infantile temper tantrums, which need no description, are sure signs of anger. Sleeping problems, such as being unable to sleep for long without interruption, may be as well. The child whom parents complain is fussy, the child who's difficult if not impossible to soothe, is often expressing anger and needs attention.

## CAUSES OF DEVELOPMENTAL ANGER
## IN TODDLERHOOD

Sometimes known as the Terrible Twos, this time in a child's life actually lasts from approximately a year and a half to three years and is marked by the greater mobility that comes with walking. As the ability to walk and increasing mental skills develop, issues of independence and separation arise. Toddlerhood is really only terrible for those caretakers who interpret the signs of blossoming independence as hints of a monster in the making and fail to understand the fear and helplessness that go along with the conflicts inherent in the new growth.

It's true that a child who's moving from the consuming dependence of infancy toward the establishment of a separate, more proficient self can appear unruly, defiant, and frequently angry, but these are normal responses to the ambivalence a child feels when he still needs a parent, even as he also begins to explore the world on his own.

*Soon after he mastered walking, Jimmy began having mini-tantrums that baffled his mother. He'd always had an even disposition, but at about seventeen months, this changed. Repeatedly, he insisted on walking away from his mother to touch an object he'd spotted across the room or to get a closer look at a neighbor who'd dropped in, for example, but then he'd shoot a dark look back at her and lapse into an angry outburst. This subsided only when she picked him up.*

*Jimmy's mother was a well-meaning and attentive caretaker, but she couldn't understand her son's behavior. I explained that Jimmy's angry feelings were a response to the normal toddler's dilemma: Am I now an autonomous agent or still a dependent infant? If I move away from Mom, will she still be there when I need her?*

*When Jimmy's mother understood this, and empathized with her son's conflict, she was able to strike the right balance between allowing him freedom and reassuring him of her continuing presence. For a few weeks, she trailed after him when he moved away, staying within closer range, but not so close that he felt inhibited. Jimmy no longer needed his angry squalls to communicate the inner helplessness he felt.*

Even under the best circumstances, toddlerhood tends to feel more like a battlefield to parents than the relative serenity of infancy. As a child's autonomy grows, a parent must necessarily set limits. The word "no"—from caretaker and child—echoes from every corner of the house during this stage of growth. A formerly docile child may quite suddenly appear to be in constant and open rebellion. Parents have asked me, at this stage in their child's life, if they have a prospective psychopath on their hands.

Probably one of the most helpful ways parents can

cope with these angry feelings is not take them personally. Remember, they are signs of growth. We're more likely to take them in stride if we recognize that beneath our child's maddeningly strong-willed posture lie feelings of helplessness and fear.

For a toddler, there's a large gap between what he thinks he can accomplish and his actual abilities. Looking around his expanding world, he sees older siblings and adults doing all sorts of inviting things and expects he'll be able to do them as well. He has no notion that skills increase gradually, through practice; he doesn't know that perfection is elusive, even for adults. So he tries something new and is rudely awakened to the knowledge of failure.

In addition, the toddler frequently clashes with vigilant and concerned parents. He may not do this (it's dangerous); he can't go in there (it's out of our sight); he shouldn't play with that (it belongs to someone else). No wonder angry feelings are so common in these neophyte explorers.

Also, the toddler's mental capacities often outstrip her relatively limited ability to communicate. She simply doesn't yet have the words at her command, an additional source of frustration.

*Mary was another one of those delightful babies, easy to please, ready to nap when put down, "just so beautiful to see with people," according to her parents. Then she hit the two-and-a-half-year mark and it was as though a dark cloud had settled over her head. She began throwing what-*

*ever she could get her hands on. She frequently responded to her parents with a defiant "NO." They were stymied by this transformation.*

*Obviously, Mary was a bright, curious, perceptive child. Her language skills were perfectly fine for her age. Still, they hadn't quite caught up with her other superior mental capacities. She felt frustrated and mad.*

*When her parents, through close observation and anticipating their daughter's needs, began to label these needs with simple new words, Mary's anger began to dissipate. After a few months, her language skills caught up with her other capacities, and the rest of her Two's weren't terrible at all.*

## Toilet Training

Traditionally, toilet training has been viewed as the quintessential arena of early power struggles, a major force in determining character. During my psychiatric training, it was certainly designated as such. My own experience with children hasn't confirmed this. Toilet training doesn't have to be a battle.

We should remember that, unless there are serious neurological problems, all children eventually learn to control their bladders and bowels. This natural bodily function shouldn't cause parents excessive worry. If children are living in a patient household, they're proud of accomplishing this developmental step and eager to receive the parental approval it brings.

Many of us may view toilet training as a measuring stick: Is our child where she ought to be on the growth charts? How is she doing compared to her peers? Is she as cooperative and civil as we'd like? Just how much power and ability do we have as parents?

This approach to toilet training is almost bound to lead to angry struggles as parents attempt to impose their own wills and schedules on the toddler, and the struggle can be fierce. This struggle is often just another in a long series of battles over power and control between parent and child. The child already feels helpless and angry and uses the contest over the potty to express it.

## Sharing

Now in more frequent contact with peers, the toddler may be asked to share toys or food, to await his or her turn, to let another child intrude on what has previously been the toddler's exclusive territory. A parent can often tell that a new playmate has arrived by the despairing screams from the sandbox. The toddler already there is anticipating the heist of his pail or shovel by the interloper, and he's mad.

Parents may also worry about other parents' judging their child's generosity and about how it reflects on them. Unwittingly, they may pressure their children unduly in this area. Toddlers aren't necessarily ready to understand the concept of sharing. Orders to share from a well-meaning parent may very well increase the anger a child feels at having to share in the first place.

The concept of sharing should be introduced slowly, by showing toddlers that sharing is a two-way street. Parents can be role models in this, indicating their own willingness to share with their youngster, while at the same time making clear that certain valuable items needn't be shared. They can also let a child know ahead of time—before a social activity—what kinds of things may have to be shared with other children.

## Signs of Anger in Toddlerhood

Toddlers have more tools at their command than do infants—both physical and mental—to express their anger. They are also increasingly involved in seeking independence and testing the limits that others set. Defiance and stubbornness frequently make their debut during this phase of a child's life. The toddler lurches across the room and pulls the cushion from one of the dining room chairs. Her mother picks it up from the floor and places it back on the chair. The toddler approaches once more, grabs for the cushion and hauls it onto the floor. The mother repeats her action. The toddler heads again for the chair. Does this seem familiar? It's the kind of dance that could go on all day between parent and toddler.

Temper tantrums occur during all developmental

stages, but during toddlerhood, the global outburst of infancy becomes more specific. Perhaps the child's environment is now the target, such as banging a toy on furniture or throwing a treasured object. It may be a particular person who's the target. A bite may be administered to the annoying aunt who insists on picking up the child when he'd rather be left alone to explore. Toddlers also begin to push and hit when necessary.

Food throwing is a common angry expression: haven't most parents received a splat of something from a toddler? So is dumping household objects— the books on lower bookcase shelves, wastebaskets, the various treasures placed on tables around the house, or vases of flowers.

A child who resists toilet training may well be expressing anger, and so may the one who smears feces on the wall, floor, or self. Sleep disturbances at this age, as at any other, often indicate anger, and dreams that frighten and wake up toddlers are possible signs of angry feelings as well.

## CAUSES OF DEVELOPMENTAL ANGER IN THE PRESCHOOLER

By the age of three, a child has generally established the physical, social, cognitive, and communication skills that make him feel like more of a person in his own right. He's able to be on his own, away from a primary caretaker, for part of the day. The beginning of school or preschool further strengthens the sense that being separated from his mother doesn't threaten his tie to her. He becomes increasingly able to go into the outside world with security and confidence. Still, there are issues at home and beyond it that produce feelings of helplessness and anger in children three to five years old.

Contacts with peers and new adults—such as teachers and other children's parents—increase rapidly during this stage. Certain facts of life are driven home to a child: there are other children in the world; some are as good as I am; some even compete with me; some aren't so nice; some pay attention to me, some don't; some like someone else better than they do me; there is only one teacher filling the needs of many children; the teacher doesn't always smooth the way for me like Mom does; the teacher has her own expectations about my conduct and productivity; the way I sometimes get what I want from Dad doesn't get me anywhere with other grown-ups at their houses; they tell me still other things I can and can't do. Imagine how it feels to confront these aspects of involvement with the larger world and you'll be able to understand that a child's feelings of frustration and helplessness may often be expressed as anger.

*Alice, who was four, was somewhat delayed in her development and still struggling with issues of separation. Instead of visiting other children's houses, she always insisted they come to hers.*

*This irritated some of the other children's parents
and the kids started to comment about it as well.
If Alice was forced to go to someone else's house,
she would rebel against the rules and try to draw
the other youngsters into mischief. When Alice's
mother was informed, she'd confront her daughter, who always denied everything. Gradually, Alice's invitations dwindled and she ended up as
something of an outcast.*

*Alice's mother had recently gone through a dif-
ficult divorce and was suffering from great anxiety over her own separation. This, in turn,
induced Alice's feelings of helplessness because
her mother unconsciously conveyed—through
pained looks and a worried tone—messages that
Alice shouldn't leave her side. Alice had become
convinced that her place was at home, and by
staying there she could also avoid the guilt and
concern of leaving her mother alone.*

*Understanding this gave the mother a clearer
grasp of why her daughter was angry and bent
on manipulating circumstances so that she could
stay at home. The mother, thereafter, talked to
other adults about her own feelings, and made
sure her daughter understood that going out
meant having a good time, not hurting her.*

*Robert was so defiant in nursery school that the
school administrator demanded a special parent-
teacher conference in which Robert's parents
heard their son described by various school per-*

sonnel as "strong-willed," "aggressive," "self-centered," and "overbearing." An only child, Robert had grown up in an affluent home where the household help did virtually everything for him. He'd assumed—and why wouldn't he?—that was the way life worked. Discovering otherwise made him angry.

When his parents assigned their son some minor chores at home and made a concerted effort to diminish the pampering he received, Robert's behavior at school improved.

Sarah's mother noticed that her daughter was sometimes very cranky and irritable when she picked her up from a twice-weekly gymnastics session; other times she seemed fine. Sarah's coach was also puzzled. Finally, the two of them were able to piece together the reason. Sarah's anger occured only when Jennie, another four-year-old, was present. Jennie was a very assertive child, and she overshadowed Sarah, who was used to having this particular spotlight on her. Sarah's sense of being eclipsed made her angry. A bit of increased attention from the coach helped to diminish her anger.

Life at home also has its share of conflicts for three- to five-year-olds. Perhaps one of the most common anger-inducers that children encounter during the preschool years is the arrival of a sibling.

This much-discussed event, eagerly anticipated by the parents, arouses the preschooler's excitement and curiosity as well. Once the baby arrives, however, the older child feels the focus shift from her and witnesses the attention lavished on the newcomer. This can't help but cause some anger, implying, as it does, a threat to the relationship between the parents and the preschooler.

It's during the preschool phase that the well-known Oedipal conflict supposedly rears its head as well. Central to Freud's thinking—and to many who have followed him—this is the time when a child "falls in love" with the parent of the opposite sex, thus becoming the jealous rival of the parent of the same sex. Freud considered the resolution of this conflict the primary determinant of future healthy development. He believed the conflict was successfully resolved when the child renounced the possessive love for the parent of the opposite sex and the hostile competition with the parent of the same sex. Such a resolution led to a normal life.

Contrary to Freudian doctrine, I don't believe the Oedipal conflict holds the key to a child's future. Certainly, behavior in children may be marked by erotic jealousy and possessiveness, but I don't consider these normal aspects of growth and development. These, and the angry episodes that occur between father and son or mother and daughter during this period, usually have other causes, such as those I've cited previously.

## Signs of Anger in Preschoolers

Some fairly elemental expressions of anger still appear during this stage. Biting, for example, hasn't passed, by any means. Now the child has a greater array of physical skills, and they may be used to attack. What may have been a nip on the ankle of the annoying aunt a year ago, for example, may now be flat-out hitting, kicking, pushing, shoving, even tackling.

As the toddler emerges into the preschooler, her angry "NO!" develops into a fuller statement of anger: "I hate you," "You're mean," or "I won't." Children of this age also become increasingly adept at angry arguments, and they don't hesitate to use direct threats or scolding against their parents or other youngsters.

In reaction to greater parental expectations, preschoolers may express anger by behavior that's explicitly contrary to our wishes. This takes the defiance and stubbornness of the toddler a step farther. Deliberate disobedience is common.

For example, you ask your daughter to play with the toys laid out on the floor and tell her she may not take more out of the cupboard; you leave the room briefly and when you return, it is strewn with the forbidden toys. Your son knows the meaning of quiet hour at nursery school, but he continues to talk and has to leave the room. The next day, at the same time, he insists on talking again. When toilet-trained children begin to backslide in this area, it may be a sign of anger.

From preschool age onward, angry children often become accident-prone. A childhood friend of mine injured himself whenever his mother went away for any period of time, always turning up at our house for treatment. Before he began kindergarten, he took a couple of nasty falls and once stuck a bean up his nose that had to be removed by a doctor. Later on, his injuries included a broken arm and fingers crushed in a garage door. He was angry. I'll discuss the accident-prone syndrome in detail later on.

Lying may begin at this age, also indicating anger. The lies aren't very accomplished—the child above, for instance, may deny to his mother that he talked during quiet hour—but they shouldn't be ignored, for they often indicate some anger.

## CAUSES OF DEVELOPMENTAL ANGER IN SCHOOL AGE CHILDREN

When children become old enough to go to school, the world away from home assumes even greater importance. Now the child spends an entire day apart from a parent or other caretaker. Adjusting to school is a big challenge in itself, as are other situations that go along with it. Children join clubs in school and get involved in other activities; they participate in athletics; or they may go off to camp during the summer. Competition enters the picture.

Competitiveness is normal and, when it's healthy, it causes kids to improve their skills and leads them to feelings of mastery and heightened self-esteem. Often, however, when they first enter the competitive arena, children feel inadequate, perhaps hesitant to join in, or fearful of failing. They have no idea yet how they're going to measure up to their peers. These uncertainties and their accompanying sense of helplessness frequently lead to the expression of anger. It's common to see children responding at first to these challenges with sulky withdrawal, superaggressiveness, or naked grandiosity, until they learn their own level of competence.

*Eight-year-old Gerald loved to play tennis with his family and had for some years. When he entered the fourth grade, he felt sure that this experience would make him a much better player than his classmates. On the first day of the recreational tennis hour at school, he leapt out of bed yowling about his tennis prowess; he kept up the bragging during morning recess. By the time he actually played, he seemed almost intoxicated with anticipation. He was defeated, however, by another "pro." This enraged him; he wanted to stay home from school the next day, and couldn't stop giving various excuses for his poor performance for over a week.*

*His rage abated, though, as he played daily*

*with the other kids and became familiar with*
*their skills. He learned that he was a good player,*
*but not number one, and didn't need to be.*

Hand in hand with competition goes the issue of
peer acceptance. Although this becomes even more
obvious during the teen years, school age children
are not immune to social jockeying. Who are the
leaders, who the followers? Cliques begin forming,
and they are of intense importance to children. Will
they be part of the in group? Will they be chosen for
a particular activity? Are they good enough to be accepted? Feelings of inferiority and fears of exclusion
or rejection lead to lots of anger and even despair
for children of this age.

*A nine-year-old boy was brought to me for a*
*consultation because he'd reportedly been hitting*
*other children at the slightest provocation. He told*
*me that if he was teased or slighted in any way,*
*he lashed out, but that other kids always started*
*it. His detailed history revealed that he suffered*
*from intense fear of social rejection, and it was*
*no wonder.*

*Both of his parents had mixed racial back-*
*grounds. He celebrated the major holidays and*
*observed the customs of at least three different re-*
*ligions. He had, as you might imagine, a lot of*
*confusion about his identity and didn't know*
*where he fit in. Placed in a racially homogeneous*
*school environment, and anticipating rejection*

*and teasing at every turn, he felt threatened constantly. This sense of powerlessness made him angry.*

A child's conscience begins to form during this phase of development, her sense of what's right and what's wrong. Although this, too, becomes even more heightened during the teen years, conflicts arise during ages six to twelve between this private code of behavior and peer pressure. A guilty conscience can cause a lot of anger, not only at oneself but toward others as well.

*Seven-year-old Alex was caught in exactly this bind when his concerned parents brought him to me because he was no longer the cheerful, outgoing child he'd always been. Worried that he was suffering from a major depression, they described him as withdrawn, moping around the house, and suffering from guilt for reasons they couldn't discern.*

*After a few sessions, Alex admitted to me that he did feel guilty all the time, and he also felt unable to do anything about it. He'd learned some curse words from friends, he explained to me, but when he tried them out on his parents, they became furious. Obviously, he no longer said them aloud at home, but he still wanted to. He also wanted to express the feelings associated with the words. This urge clashed with his desire to live up to his parents' moral code.*

*When Alex understood that this kind of conflict was common, that he wasn't a "bad" child, and when his parents became a bit more enlightened about children and cursing and realized that it was fairly normal for Alex's age group, the anger he'd been feeling passed.*

As parents well know, school performance is an area that can be downright combustible. Pressures associated with school achievement generate more anger in children than any other factor during this time in their lives. Not only do parental expectations cause angry feelings, many children also have learning disabilities that are hard to detect. These difficulties may be transient or ongoing, but in either case they cause great pain and shame. Anger accompanies these feelings.

*Eddie was a classic wiseguy in class, constantly talking to kids nearby, acting up, and disturbing the teacher and the order in his classroom. Not a good student, he'd decided to become a prize troublemaker instead. When I saw him and recommended some educational diagnostic testing, it became clear that he had some rather serious learning disabilities.*

*Eddie knew he wasn't up to the work that school presented, but he didn't know why and he couldn't do anything about it on his own. Of course he was angry, and his behavior showed it. When he received remedial teaching, his academic record improved and his anger began to dissipate as well.*

## Signs of Anger in School Age Children

Angry behavior displayed by preschool children doesn't miraculously change when they enter school; some of these expressions of anger remain. New expressions of anger may also appear and poor school performance is a primary, although indirect, one. This may indicate anger a child feels at parents, teachers, or both.

Various kinds of antisocial behavior signal anger in school age children. Stealing, from parents, other kids, or the corner candy store is an example. Lying persists and grows more polished. You may notice that your child has acquired a general air of sneakiness. Violent acts toward others, bullying, and verbal aggression are strong signals that a child is angry.

Two other signs of anger that are less easy to spot are overly competitive or overly ambitious behavior, whether in school, on the playground, or at home. Since the ability to compete and the desire to achieve can be perfectly healthy, how does a parent know when to be concerned? It can be a difficult distinction to make.

Although not foolproof, the best test of whether or not your child's competitiveness should give you pause might be to gauge her reaction to losing. If it's extreme and long-lasting, it may indicate underlying anger. As for overambition, if your child's need for accomplishment has a driven quality—if it seems to be a matter of life and death—it's most likely connected to anger. Showing off, which becomes easily recognizable during these years, could be related to either of the above as well.

Sleep remains a sensitive indicator of anger throughout childhood—and beyond, for that matter. At this age, insomnia and nightmares are the most common disturbances.

## CAUSES OF DEVELOPMENTAL ANGER IN THE TEEN YEARS

Adolescence is filled with challenges as teenagers seek to establish their independence, social competence, and sexual identity. They also begin to make academic and vocational choices that will have great bearing on their futures.

This phase of development begins with puberty. Physical changes to the structure and function of teenagers' bodies cause them anxiety. Frequently this anxiety focuses on timing: Susie already has her period; what's wrong with me? I can't believe Roger's shaving and I'm still hairless all over.

Extreme self-consciousness results. Never again in life will the concern with physical appearance be so concentrated or so all-consuming. Teens aren't yet used to their new bodies and they're plagued by doubts about them. They can literally spend hours getting a lock of hair just right, adjusting a shirt collar, or matching their jewelry and outfit. A small facial blemish may make them want to hide in their room for days. The slightest sense of being "off" in any way, of not being attractive enough, can trigger a barrage of angry expressions ranging from mild disgust or irritation to full-blown tantrums. Often, these tantrums reach their peak just as a teenager is about to leave the house to go out with friends or on a date.

Sexual feelings, and the possibilities of sexual experimentation, come with puberty. These sexual matters are also fraught with anxiety, as well as excitement and sometimes guilt. Children frequently feel at the mercy of their bodies, inducing an overall sense of helplessness that is commonly expressed by anger.

All of the above—pubertal changes, concern with physical appearance, and sexual feelings—are reflected in the social arena. Children worry about fitting in and being sought after. Does the opposite sex find them attractive? Does their own sex accept them? Are they popular? As popular as so-and-so? Falling short socially carries great weight for the teenager. Social rejections, real or imagined, are a major source of anger for kids this age. My own rule of thumb is to assume that unexplained anger in a teenager stems from feelings of social rejection, unless or until proven otherwise.

The issue of independence is as central for the teenager as it is for the toddler, although adolescents operate on a much more advanced intellectual, moral, and developmental level. Teenagers evolve by arguing with parents or other adults, defying them, and rebelling against them. Though normal, this is often an angry process. Sometimes the issues are petty, sometimes profound, but the arguments are almost always passionate. Moody, volatile teenagers often respond as though everything were a matter of life and death—and to them, it feels that way. As though they were auditioning for adulthood, they try on different roles in an effort to create a solid identity for themselves. These rehearsals can often confuse parents but are no need for worry.

*Recently, I ran into a neighbor's son on the street. As we walked, he asked with great sincerity whether psychiatry could really help people.*

*"Yes," I answered. "How come you're asking?"*

*"Oh, I was just wondering," he said.*

*After I made sure that he wasn't really seeking help for a problem of his own, we went on talking.*

*"But basically," he continued, "medicine's a way of getting rich, right? I mean, more and more the world's becoming two groups, rich and poor. And if you're a doctor, you know which group you're going to end up in."*

*"Maybe that's the motive for some people," I replied.*

*The walk didn't last much longer but even so, by its end he'd managed to challenge a few more of my assumed values. Each of his retorts to me grew a little angrier than the last.*

This wasn't an unusual encounter. A teenager needs to test the limits, with all the give-and-take that implies. Such seemingly hostile exchanges are normal parts of development. Outgrowing dependence and becoming a separate individual is accomplished, in part, by pushing the limits and responding angrily to limit-setting. Even when the teenager's response includes contempt and belittlement of adult values, there's not necessarily any cause for alarm. These expressions of anger are the psychological equivalent of working out in order to develop certain muscles—if you don't exercise them, they'll never grow stronger.

In later adolescence, staring the future in the face may also provoke feelings of helplessness, as teenagers contemplate further separation from their parents and the possibility of being on their own. Perhaps they're also being urged to make choices about education or a vocation, and they are feeling ill-equipped to do so. These pressures frequently arouse anger in kids.

## Signs of Anger in the Teen Years

Teenagers and anger can be synonymous in parents' minds. Often there's nothing secret about it. Who needs a so-called "expert" to point out the various ways teens express anger? parents may ask themselves. They get a dose of it every day. Teenagers are able to use the full range of their now well-developed mental and verbal abilities and their own quite acute perceptions as well.

Teenage anger has a flavor all its own. Adolescents are masters of the derisive, sarcastic, contemptuous remark. They frequently dish out withering scorn, and no one receives larger portions of this than parents. The profanity they discovered during their younger years blossoms during the teenage years. Rebellion against parental rules sometimes seems almost automatic.

Teenagers are capable of long-winded, well-reasoned displays of anger—arguments, lectures, harangues—that tax even the most serene among us. They may be given to bravura emotional displays. The antisocial, passive-aggressive behaviors observed in younger kids may continue and become more organized.

Despite its often explosive and obvious nature, teenage anger sometimes is expressed in subtler, more disguised ways. The well-known moodiness of adolescence may signal anger, and depression nearly always does. Teenagers suffer from insomnia, as younger children do, but oversleeping may be the more likely manifestation of anger among adolescents.

Keep in Mind:

- Anger in the course of development is normal, expectable, and actually helpful.
- Each new phase of childhood brings unique challenges for children to master, which often causes lots of frustration.

- Each child expresses anger in unique ways.
- It is your responsibility to become familiar not only with your particular child's anger expression but also to be aware of issues in development that might be giving rise to this feeling.

Having surveyed the phases of development we are aware that every child confronts obstacles throughout infancy to adolescence. With each expected developmental hurdle comes frustration, stress, and anger.

Remember, human interactions are another source of growth and frustration. The next section will discuss this important area in more detail.

# CHAPTER FIVE

# Interpersonal Anger in Children

Most parents and other adults consciously mean well when they're dealing with children, but none of us is perfect. At one time or another, we all cause anger in other members of our families. I'd venture to say this probably happens daily for most of us and, of course, it happens with our children.

Often we're unaware of how we make kids mad. Operating on the principle that it's up to us to educate our children about certain things, to do what's best for them in the long run, to expose them to "character-building" experiences, we sometimes treat them as if they were immune to our behavior. How much do they really take in? we may rationalize. Won't they be grateful one day for what we've instilled in them? The things we do for our children in their best interests may also cause them to feel helpless and angry.

Although all of us anger our children sometimes, and this is usually a benign passing event, we do need to be aware of what causes the anger. It's only when our actions go on in unrecognized fashion for a while, and our child's angry reactions to us aren't appreciated as such, do real troubles begin.

As before, if you recognize yourself in some of the following anger-inducing situations, don't be alarmed. Generally, common human foibles lie at the root of these and, if we're willing, we can change them.

### THE MAJOR INTERPERSONAL ANGER INDUCERS

- Unfair treatment
- Making a child feel unwanted
- Cold treatment
- Neglect
- Unkept promises
- Inconsistency
- Hypocrisy
- Creating a double bind
- Inducing guilt feelings
- Overprotection
- Teasing
- Pessimism
- Allowing the child to continually fail
- Disparagement
- Arbitrary exercise of power
- Intimidation, humiliation, and bullying
- Excessive parental demands

- Unjust comparisons
- Using the child to fulfill parental needs
- An angry household

## Unfair Treatment

Unfair treatment makes all kids mad. A certain amount of this is unavoidable. Life isn't necessarily fair and, sooner or later, this is brought home to all of us. There are some specific parental actions, however, such as unjust punishments, arbitrary decisions, or treating siblings as equals regardless of age, that produce helpless feelings in children, and accompanying anger.

Parents are the court of last resort. When Dad, because he's had a bad day, says no to what seems a reasonable request, a child is generally stuck with the decision. Perhaps, simply because it's easier for the parents to lump the two together, a ten-year-old child misses out on an activity that's been forbidden to his seven-year-old sister. Where does the ten-year-old go to appeal his case? It doesn't matter if the treatment is unfair; kids are powerless to change it, and this causes anger.

We should always step back to gauge our fairness, especially when complaints on this score are frequent.

## Feeling Unwanted

Occasionally, a parent may tell a child that he's an unwelcome burden, but more often, this message is sent indirectly by ignoring him or by arguing with a spouse in front of a child about the travails of child rearing ("Do you think it's easy for me to deal with him all day? I'd rather be running things at your shop").

A child will also feel unwanted by a parent who constantly turns him over to caretakers or regularly farms him out to friends or relatives. Kids know the difference between a busy parent and one who's trying to avoid them. Another certain way to make a child feel unwanted is to treat him as a nuisance, greeting any request with obvious annoyance, making clear how aggravating it is ("What do you want *now?*" "I thought I told you not to bother me").

Neglect produces feelings of being unwanted, even though it's predicated on the absurd, but not uncommon, notion that children don't really notice much, anyway. We should never underestimate the sensitivity and perceptiveness children have about what goes on around them. Unwittingly, we may make a child feel unwanted by ignoring her communications, not paying sufficient attention to her feelings about various situations, and neglecting her needs for nurturing, discipline, and rewards for a job well done.

Few parents feel at all times that they don't want

a child; more often, if that feeling arises, it waxes and wanes, depending on a parent's current problems. It is nearly always the case that a parent has other problems that seem overwhelming at the time. When such a feeling does occur, though, it's important not to act it out. Remembering problems that were resolved in the past is a good way of getting present problems in perspective and avoiding this type of hurtful behavior toward our children.

## Cold Treatment

When a parent doesn't display warm and accepting feelings toward a child and is excessively controlled, chilliness pervades the household. This absence of emotion, which a child is helpless to change, makes him feel isolated and ineffectual, as well as angry ("I may as well not be here, since nothing I do makes any difference"). This kind of blight can be especially damaging.

People vary in the degree of emotion they express and the ways they display it, but even someone who's generally reserved can also relate to others with warmth. If that capacity doesn't exist, then there's often a deeper problem, such as depression, which can most likely be treated.

## Unkept Promises

Breaking promises makes kids mad and, quite innocently, we've probably all fallen into this trap at one time or another. Often, we promise something in order to resolve a tense situation or to get ourselves off the hook. We don't think through whether or not we're likely to live up to such pledges. Again, parents are the ones with the power to say yes or no. What can a child do if we decide to renege? When we do renege on a promise, it's best to explain our reasons and, especially when kids over five are involved, to give a time when the matter can be discussed again. This is almost sure to decrease the anger that has been generated, if not immediately, within a short time. Most of all, we should develop the habit of hesitating before making a promise to be sure we can carry it out.

## Inconsistency

Inconsistency is maddening for children. Ideally, because kids need to know what they can count on, all parents would faithfully hold to certain basic attitudes and behavior. Rigidity or inflexibility aren't necessary or helpful, but a generally consistent application of standards for acceptable behavior is. If a misdeed is punished one time and ignored the next, a child is left confused and angry.

The younger the child, the more important consistency is. Up to the ages of seven or eight, kids themselves are in such flux that parents have to adhere to rules about such things as bedtimes and meals.

To be a consistent parent, you should:

- Think out, beforehand, how to deal with certain everyday situations. Routines for starting the day, how to come and go from the house, and bedtime activities are good examples.
- Never change a basic rule in the house under the influence of pressure, without first taking time to think it out—even if that means having an angry child wait for a final decision. Parental behavior will appear consistent and predictable, although sometimes very frustrating. This thinking through on the part of the parent decreases the opportunities for impulsive decisions and the forgetting of past positions.
- Try for consistency in the display of feelings. Children are very affected by unanticipated changes in feeling tones and behaviors of parents. One of the most damaging aspects of parental substance abuse is the unpredictability of parents' emotions while under the influence.

## Hypocrisy

Nothing makes children more angry than hypocrisy. This is a duplicitous way of relating in which a person says one thing and means another. Kids seem to have impeccable radar for picking up hypocrisy. Usually, extremely hypocritical people are riddled with conflicts they've attempted to solve by putting an acceptable face on things, but their true feelings all too often show through. A parent may attempt to live with minor conflicts in as smooth a fashion as possible by not practicing what he preaches. Intense hypocrisy provokes great feelings of helplessness in children. Kids are forced to accept the surface version of things while sensing that what's underneath is more real. This leads them to lose faith and trust in parental figures as well as invoking much anger.

## Double Bind

Related to hypocrisy is the parental behavior that creates what's called a double bind. This ensnares the helpless child in a trap from which she can't escape. It occurs when parents prompt a child to behave, think, or feel one way, while at the same time sending a message that this conflicts with another, and different, parental desire. Obviously, these parents suffer from great conflicts themselves, and no matter how hard they try to do what they believe is right, their conflicting feelings seep through.

*Mary's mother constantly asked her sixteen-year-old daughter for details about her social life, appearing to support and encourage her dating and social success. Who asked Mary out? What did she enjoy doing on dates? Was one friend closer or more popular or smarter than another? Yet every time Mary announced that she had a date or was going out with friends, a look of despair would cross her mother's face and she'd begin worrying about the logistics of the activity.*

*She'd seem actually frightened by the prospect of Mary going off on her own and weakening the bond between the two of them, betraying her own feelings of loneliness and isolation.*

*The mother was a single parent who had few friends or social outlets of her own. She both relished vicariously the details of her daughter's relationships and hated to see her going off on her own. Eventually, when she became involved with activities at a neighborhood center and began to develop social contacts of her own, she stopped putting Mary in an impossible, maddening situation.*

To avoid the anger complications of both hypocrisy and the double bind, we should exercise great care in delivering a straightforward message, even if this means cutting out ancillary messages that you want to get across. Knowing and planning what we want to say, being patient, and speaking slowly and in an uncomplicated fashion allows us to deliver a simple communication and decreases the risk that we will send confusing messages.

## Guilt

Producing guilt in a child also produces anger. Usually, parents resort to this when they feel powerless to change a situation by any other means. The particular circumstances might be difficult for a parent to handle, or perhaps he feels generally ineffectual due to personal problems such as depression, low self-esteem, or a sense of chronic failure.

A child can be made to feel guilty by such verbal expressions as: "You're such a disappointment to me." "You ought to be ashamed of yourself." "It hurts me every time you do that." Guilt also can be instilled nonverbally: by a deep and meaningful sigh, by head-shaking that's obviously meant to convey incredulity at a child's behavior, or simply by a grimace of hurt or disappointment.

No matter how a parent produces guilt, the end result is that the child feels bad and dislikes herself for having been a disappointment or having done something hurtful. She feels angry both at herself and at the parent who's made her feel guilty.

When a parent's sense of empowerment increases through actions such as work success, straightening out a poor relationship with someone, or getting help for deeper problems, the need to use guilt to control situations generally diminishes.


## Overprotection

Overprotective behavior by a parent doesn't grow out of a simple desire to shield a child from reasonable danger. In fact, its exaggerated nature—excessive worrying, doting, insulating the child from outside factors, issuing dire warnings, and inducing fear—suggests that other motives are operating. It used to be assumed that this behavior usually covered up an essentially hostile attitude toward a child.

That may be true in some cases and not others. Whatever parental need overprotectiveness represents, it always leaves a child feeling helpless, angry, and intimidated.

This is especially true when parents fuss and agonize over a child's health, worrying about the burgeoning cold of a playmate, for example, taking a child's temperature at the slightest provocation or overemphasizing the pitfalls of improper sanitary measures, which generally feel burdensome to kids anyway. The upshot of such hovering is that the child develops a feeling of vulnerability, a sense that he lives in a perilous world. He feels fragile and powerless to combat the ravages of the illnesses no doubt bearing down on him. This can make him very angry.

## Teasing

Teasing by a parent, authority figure, or anyone else can arouse great anger in children. Most often this is just simply playful jibing, but sometimes this behavior is sadistic and makes a child feel helplessly enraged, especially when it is done frequently. Most kids don't feel able to fight back adequately against "friendly" digs and they sense they're at an unusual disadvantage.

I think it's a good idea to refrain from teasing on any level until we are sure that the particular child can flow with it. If we find ourselves always teasing, we should absolutely refrain until we can find out more about why we need to do this.

## Scapegoating

It's not uncommon for a child to become a scapegoat, especially in families that have active, ongoing conflicts. When parents can't focus squarely on the true problems in the household, they may blame a child, who's usually innocent, for whatever goes wrong. This can be particularly insidious because the parents are often completely unconscious of what they're doing and because the child may very well come to believe that she is, in fact, responsible.

There are many complex reasons why a particular child might be chosen for this role, such as his particular temperament, his physical appearance, or even his or her gender.

Scapegoating, which persists for long periods of time, not only produces great helplessness and rage but eventually can deform the personality as well. It often results in a long-standing embittered feeling of being victimized.

## Pessimism

This is a very troubling attitude for children to encounter. An adult can be pessimistic for a variety of reasons: perhaps he's depressed or resigned to a life of minimal happiness; maybe he feels trapped and overwhelmed by certain aspects of life, such as a poor marriage or an ongoing illness; or he might just be a wet blanket by nature, someone who always looks on the dark side. Whatever the cause, pessimism puts a terrible damper on the hopefulness of youth. It creates a negative and forbidding atmosphere, feelings of apprehension, and it angers anyone who's constantly exposed to it, especially a child who's just beginning to recognize all of life's possibilities.

## Allowing Continual Failure

Allowing continual failure in a child is an indirect or passive anger-inducer. This may be hard to identify, because it can masquerade as a benign or even compassionate approach toward a child who isn't doing well: for example, the anxious preschooler who's allowed to cry each day before nursery school without an attempt to discover the cause of her distress, the child who's the butt of jokes and teasing at school but receives no parental counsel on how to handle it, or a teenager whose increasing experimentation with substances is viewed as a passing phase. When a child persistently fails to accomplish a task or is doing things that clearly are detrimental, parental intervention is called for. Letting a child continue to fail is a type of neglect.

*When seven-year-old Lester was brought to me, he was a bundle of angry behaviors. He argued about everything, was given to temper outbursts, and was depressed as well. His teachers had been noting for some time that his reading lagged behind his classmates', and he'd virtually stopped participating in school. His father had decided, however, that Les was simply mad, and the reading problem was part of "an attitude" on his son's part.*

*When testing showed that Les had a bona fide reading disability, his father confided that he had the same problem and had been ashamed of it for years. Secretly, he'd hoped his son wasn't suffering from it, and Les's father was angry at this reminder of his own painful past. In order to protect his self-esteem and, unknowingly, to punish Les for causing him pain, he'd left his son to flounder unaided.*

## Disparagement

Any victim of disparagement will most likely feel angry, and children are no exception. Interestingly, though, they can often become angry when they hear a parent put down someone else. I had dinner recently with a couple who brought along their thirteen-year-old daughter. When the father, who was prone to belittling others, made disparaging comments about a neighbor, I could see his daughter squirming with discomfort and anger. I imagine that she identified with the neighbor.

## The Arbitrary Exercise of Power

Children need their parents to exert a certain amount and kind of authority. Unfortunately, in the hands of some parents, wielding authority becomes an arbitrary exercise of power. These parents believe that such behavior will administer a good upbringing that teaches children to be respectful. Most likely, this is how the parents themselves were raised. They usually haven't given much thought to the subtler aspects of human behavior.

Such an authoritarian posture consists of making rigid demands on children and leaves almost no room for questioning and dialogue. Children's opinions are ignored. They have no opportunity to learn at home that there's room for negotiation in most of life's interchanges.

Parents have the greatest power over very young children. With infants, this power borders on the absolute and necessary, but even very early in life, it's a good idea to begin to sense, ask for, and respect a child's input as often as possible; what direction a toddler's walking in; the type of game a child wants to play; and later on, with older kids, the negotiation of curfews and activities.

## Intimidation, Humiliation, and Bullying

People who themselves feel rather powerless may relate to others by intimidation, humiliation, and bullying. They try to get their way by attempting to exert sheer force on others. A child can't possibly hold his or her own against such tactics from a parent. Inevitably, the child will experience feelings of inferiority, shame, fear, and overall helplessness. This, as always, produces anger.

A parent who asserts his will over a child in these ways may do so overtly or operate more indirectly by setting up an array of negative experiences for the child, such as blatant failure or public embarrassment. At best, this sort of sadistic behavior may be a passing phenomenon, prompted by a difficult time in the parent's life. If it's an ongoing issue, one should consider being certain that children are kept away from this person as much as possible.

## Excessive Parental Demands

Every child has complaints about parental demands. They seem to go with the territory and are to be expected. A parent who's excessively demanding is most likely perfectionistic, holds impossibly high standards for her own behavior, and she applies those same standards to her child. No youngster will be able to meet these impossible goals, and she'll be left feeling helpless and angry as a result of her failure.

Parents who make perfectionistic demands commonly focus on how a child dresses, performs in school or on the athletic field, whether or not she's accepted by the right clique, keeps her room neat, and has good manners and high morals, particularly sexual ones.

Related to unrealistic parental demands, and equally enraging, is the behavior of forcing a child to do something for which he has no talent or that doesn't even interest him. Examples of this might be pushing a budding musician to go out for the football team or making a child who's fascinated by science take piano lessons. When parents push certain pursuits on their kids, it's usually because the parents themselves are interested in the activity or because they feel it's right for a child to follow a particular path. Gender often plays a role here and frequently stereotypes are invoked, such as the old notions that girls aren't supposed to be interested in science, and boys ought to pursue athletics.

## Unjust Comparisons

When there's more than one child in a household, it's hard for parents to avoid comparing siblings to one another. It is, however, well worth making an extra effort to view each child as a separate person with unique talents and shortcomings. Otherwise, we rob a child of her individuality, a precious commodity. Who doesn't feel angry when they've had something taken away from them?

## Using the Child to Fulfill Parental Needs

Turning to a child for our own need fulfillment to an excessive degree is, unfortunately, very common. Needs such as those for companionship, nurturing, and encouragement that ought to be met by the other parent or another appropriate adult are demanded of the child. Asking a child to fulfill them turns the parent-child relationship upside down. Most commonly, these situations happen when a parent has low self-esteem and fears rejection from peers (situations that often respond well to professional help), or is going through a particularly stressful time. The child who's put in such a position over long periods feels the inherent inequity and conflict and, of course, this causes anger.

## An Angry Household

An angry household produces angry children. Probably most of us have been in at least one home like this at some point. Its distinguishing feature is that everyone yells at everyone else, no matter what the provocation. The high volume indicates a low tolerance for stress. A child in this situation doesn't have much chance to develop a healthy patience for such feelings nor to learn other ways of relating. The atmosphere makes her feel assaulted by the constant, high-pitched sound of anger. Kids who grow up in such an environment tend to be quick to anger.

This is all they've ever seen and heard, and they've learned to fight fire with fire.

> *I was once asked to observe the class behavior of a fourth-grade bully. It was pretty predictable; he aggressively tried to intimidate everyone around him in any way he could. The conference I requested afterward with the parents was no surprise either; it was essentially a contest of wills. The mother and father constantly battled each other for the floor, neither listening to the other, and their son did likewise. "If you can't beat 'em, join 'em" is the principle that operates in situations like this.*

It's not easy to change such households, as they've been molded by long histories, but no parent should accept such constant anger as normal. Children from these families are virtually doomed, at some point, to act inappropriately angry outside the home. Unless a change occurs, often professional help is necessary.

Remember:

- It's normal to produce anger in our children in any of a host of ways.
- It's important that we be knowledgeable about how we do anger our children, because only then can we control it.
- Continuous generation of anger over a long period

without attention and relief sets the stage for an anger metamorphosis.

- We can change the ways that we relate once we are sensitive to the consequences for those close to us.
- You will never be completely free of causing anger in others because this is part of being human.

# CHAPTER SIX

# Handling Anger Constructively

Because anger problems can be so detrimental to children and so long-lasting, it's important for those who have extensive contact with kids—parents, teachers, counselors, clergy, coaches, tutors, nannies, babysitters, and others—to be aware of the importance of anger issues and to attempt to deal with them in as honest and constructive a way as possible.

Some of us are fortunate enough to have had reasonably adequate anger educations in our own childhoods, enabling us to handle most of a child's angry feelings in ways that aren't destructive. Still, however competent we feel in this area, however dedicated we are to doing our best, an angry child can be upsetting. In the vast majority of us, an angry child can evoke strong feelings.

Before getting to specific ways of dealing with children's anger, it's good to keep several general principles in mind.

- Angry children can make adults angry.
- Our own problems can interfere with our management of our children's anger.
- Anger isn't necessarily personal.
- Anger is no reason to panic.

## ANGRY CHILDREN CAN MAKE ADULTS ANGRY

Even under the best circumstances, an angry child can make a parent feel angry. When we feel helpless, we become angry, almost as though the anger were contagious. If we're feeling angry, it's hard to respond to the situation helpfully.

Adult anger at children is not only normal, it's impossible to avoid. In fact, I wouldn't believe a parent who said he'd never gotten mad at his child. Either he's lying or he's completely out of touch with his feelings. Kids can be infuriating; there's no getting around that.

It's also common for parents' anger at children to run the gamut from mild irritation to murderous, if fleeting, fantasies. Haven't we all, at moments, felt that we'd like to say to our kids the equivalent of "drop dead"? Haven't we all just wanted a child to disappear—temporarily? There's nothing unusual or shameful about these feelings. They come from our sense of helplessness and frustration, the same things that induce anger in children.

When we're mad at our kids, the same principles

that apply to handling children's anger apply to our own. The first of these is to figure out the reason why we're angry. Often the cause is obvious, and we can deal with the situation in a straightforward way. When it's resolved, our angry feelings dissolve; there aren't any lingering, harmful aftereffects for us, for the child, or for our relationship. The relationship, in fact, may be strengthened by the experience.

*You've asked your daughter to clean up her room before going out on a date. The accumulating clothing, papers and books, tapes and headphones, beauty products, and other assorted teenage paraphernalia have now made it impossible to open the door more than a body's width.*

*"Sure, Mom," she answers. "No problem."*

*After she's gone, however, you find that the mess is worse than ever. You're angry, and wait up for your daughter to tell her so. You also point out that it's her responsibility to clean her room, that she shouldn't say she's going to do things and not follow through on them, and you set a deadline for the cleanup. She's a little put out, but grudgingly agrees, and you both go off to bed, no worse for wear.*

*Perhaps your son arrives home in the late afternoon one day looking stormy and immediately begins picking on his little sister, listing all the "stupid" things she's doing or has ever done. Then he says he's ready for dinner. You haven't started* cooking yet and tell him it'll be another half hour before he can eat. If he's really hungry, you add, he can get dinner started himself. He launches into something between a whine and a rant.

"I don't see why you can't at least have dinner ready when I'm hungry. You've been home for an hour. And I know you haven't been ironing my shirt like I asked you to, because I just looked in my closet and it's still not there. I mean, what good's a mother if you can't count on her to do certain things? Joey doesn't have to sort his own laundry or take his brother to the dentist. His mother does all that junk. You're just interested in your own stuff. And you're not even smart enough to help me with my math."

You'd like to say that if he wants to get into character assassination, you've got some complaints of your own about his self-centeredness, his arrogance, his disrespect. You'd like to say, "Who does he think he is?" Instead, you make yourself scarce for fifteen minutes or so and calm down.

Then you go to his room and tell him that what he said was insulting and made you angry. You're not his servant and everything in the house can't run on his schedule. Also, unlike Joey's family, in yours everyone has to pitch in. You suggest that maybe he's angry about something else and say you'd be happy to talk to him about it, but whatever's bothering him is no excuse to treat you or his little sister as he has, and *you won't permit it. When he's angry, you say, instead of lashing out at others, perhaps he ought to take some time, as you did, to get control of himself. Several hours later, when you ask if he wants to talk about why he was angry, he does.*

*You've taken your small daughter with you on a specific shopping mission to buy fabric for dining room curtains. In the store, passing the toy department, your daughter spots something she wants. You say no; she has toys she hasn't even played with yet, and you need to complete your errand.*

*"I hate you," she yells at the top of her lungs. "I never get anything. I'm leaving." And she drops the toy and runs toward the door.*

*Furious, you run after her and catch up near the exit. Taking her out to the car, you tell her that you understand how much she wanted the toy, but she couldn't have it today. You hope she won't always feel that she gets nothing. You also tell her never to run off as she did because it's dangerous. You add that it frightened and angered you. Although crying, she listens and, after you've said your piece, she goes with you to buy the fabric. When you get home, you take out one of her untouched toys and play with it together.*

Each of these children did something to make his or her parents angry. The degree of anger varied, as it does, depending on the offense and on the individual. A dirty room isn't the same as a degrading comment or demanding, embarrassing, potentially dangerous behavior in a public place. Also, some people control their anger with relative ease, while others may need time to collect themselves.

However, in all three instances, these parents handled their anger well. They knew what angered them and announced their feelings in direct, uncomplicated ways.

What they didn't do was to act out their anger destructively. They didn't throw around any big, confusing words that their child might not understand. They didn't recite long histories of past transgressions. They didn't attack or insult their children. They didn't prophesy gloomy futures for such hopeless creatures. There was no harm done. Communication and relatedness were enhanced.

Constructively handling anger at our children doesn't mean that the household will automatically be restored to a model of calm and tranquillity. Taking steps like those discussed above certainly clears the air. However, we may not immediately shake off traces of the anger; our child may sulk for a time; tension may linger in the atmosphere. Perhaps it will take some time to rekindle mutual closeness. Still, we'll know we've communicated effectively and fairly, and that our relationship with the youngster hasn't been damaged.

It's important to remember that feeling anger toward our children and expressing it isn't destructive in and of itself. Anger on our part isn't harmful, or "bad," anymore than it is for our children. It becomes a problem only when we can't handle our angry feelings constructively.

## RECOGNIZING OUR PART IN THE PROBLEM

Sometimes we may bring emotional baggage of our own to a situation confronting us that prevents us from acting constructively when face to face with an angry child. There are reasons why we get mad or overly mad that aren't always as obvious as a child's filthy room, a broken promise, denigrating remarks, or risky behavior. Sometimes it takes a little detective work to figure out what they are. Often, we find that the reasons have more to do with us than they do with our children.

Take the mother whose son was carping at her for all the things she wasn't doing. Despite his inflammatory, hurtful language, she handled the situation and her anger very capably. Let's suppose instead that her own mother has been ill, and that she's just returning from visiting her in the hospital, feeling sad, anxious, and maybe even a little guilty for leaving. Her stress tolerance might be lower than usual. The mother might not be able to take the fifteen minutes in another room to get her anger under control; she might light into her son instead, trading insults with him.

Let's assume, in the case of the mother whose daughter was demanding a toy, that she'd had a fight with her boss the day before. Her preoccupation and anxiety about losing her job might cause her to respond differently. Maybe instead of taking the child to the car for a reasoned discussion, she'd find herself yelling at the top of her lungs in the store.

All of us have times when we're drained of our usual tolerance for reasons that have nothing to do with our children. We have financial worries; a parent is sick or has just died; we're concerned about an ongoing, difficult situation at work. So we snap at our child, yell, withdraw, or overreact with scolding or criticism that's out of proportion to the event.

Most of us catch on in these cases pretty quickly. We regret them and apologize to our kids for losing our temper. Our anger was briefly out of control, and we did express it destructively, but this hardly qualifies as a major disaster. Our child's feelings may be hurt, but children are quick to forgive and to let go of lingering resentments. All of us can survive such momentary lapses without any real damage.

If we know that we're feeling strained, that our customary tolerance is at a low ebb, or that we feel angry even though we're not sure why, it's not a bad idea to give our kids a wide berth for a bit. Ideally, we might turn things over to our spouse or another caretaker while we take a break and do something that's soothing and relaxing, such as exercising, listening to music, reading, or gardening.

Just as it's important for us to discover the sources of our children's anger, in situations like these we need to probe ourselves a little more deeply, to ask ourselves some questions without being condemning or judgmental. What's really bothering us? What situations in our lives might be giving us problems? Has a coworker's passing remark earlier in the day been festering ever since? Is our job in jeopardy? Are we feeling jealous or envious of someone? Are there problems in our marriage that we've been shoving under the rug? Why haven't we made a doctor's appointment to check out that pain after meals? Any number of things could be making us angry and increase the chances that we'll be impatient with our children.

If we direct our anger at our kids inappropriately, we owe them an apology, and the sooner the better. They aren't eager to be on the outs with us—we're still the most important people in their lives.

Apologies from adults set a powerful example for children. They learn important lessons when we say we're sorry. Many things are implicit in an apology: the admission that we're not perfect, that we make mistakes, and that we can blow our cool. We can also realize our mistake and quickly rectify it.

## TRY NOT TO TAKE ANGER PERSONALLY

An angry child can also be disconcerting because the anger may very well be directed right at us, and with great intensity. Often in my practice, someone feeling helpless expresses anger at me. I want to be of assistance even while I am being screamed at, criticized, and rejected. Parents find themselves in this unenviable position all the time. In the heat of the moment, it's hard to appreciate the irony, and it's hard for most of us not to take some of this anger personally.

*Not long ago I was walking through a department store. As I neared the teenage clothing section, I heard some hair-raising screams and the following situation unfolded. A young teenager was shrieking at her mother, who was delivering clothing to a dressing room. Each new garment was criticized more vociferously than the one before, and each added to the barrage of ridicule being directed at the mother. She had no idea what to choose; was she crazy to think her daughter would wear such a thing; did she have any idea that only a major nerd would even think about wearing something so tacky; what was the matter with her?*

*The mother's exasperation increased but still she kept trying to help, despite her daughter's despair and disparagement. The mother obviously recognized her daughter's helplessness, empathized with her frustration, and understood some of the forces operating at this time in her daughter's life, the primary one being an obsession with appearance. A half hour later, I saw the two of them in the parking lot chatting away happily as though the dressing room episode had never happened.*

*A school age boy wanted a basketball like the one his older brother, now in college, had. The father said that his son could use his older brother's ball now that he was away; it seemed like a waste of money to buy a new one. The young boy got very angry and, in a raised voice, began to accuse his father of preferring the older brother.*

*Although he was the victim of this noisy onslaught, the father quietly told the boy that he understood that younger siblings often feel they play second fiddle. The father assured his son that he certainly didn't feel that way about him. Like the mother above, this father managed to withstand his child's anger without losing the capacity to appreciate the underlying issue.*

In both instances, these parents were able to resist personalizing their children's anger and responding as though it were an attack on them, even though they were the immediate targets.

## ANGER ISN'T CAUSE FOR PANIC

Parents often feel consternation about their child's anger. They think that they have to solve the child's problem immediately, if not sooner. This kind of unrealistic demand on oneself can cause a parent to panic when confronted with an angry child and to become very angry at himself as well. He feels the angry child is *his* failure.

This is an overreaction. It is not possible to solve or to anticipate all your children's problems. Perfect parenting, if such a thing even existed, doesn't consist of jumping into the breach each time a problem arises for your child. Doing so robs a child of developing his own ability to solve problems.

When handling a child's anger, keep in mind that anger can seem contagious; our tolerance for anger varies from day to day; even when we're the targets, it may have little to do with us; and it's not a cause for panic. It's a sign of helplessness and distress that will pass.

## HOW TO HANDLE CHILDREN'S ANGER

What should we do when our child's mad? Obviously, if we know the source of a child's helpless feelings, we'll want to try to take actions that will alleviate them.

But what if we're faced with a situation in which we can see that our child is angry, but the cause remains a mystery, and to make matters worse, the situation constitutes an emergency because our child is so angry that it's possible she could damage herself, others, or something around her? What do we do when things seem out of control?

## Anger First Aid

This simple-sounding measure is much harder to put into practice than it is to describe, but here's what you should do:

- Supply the necessary control.
- Suggest a cooling off or time-out period.
- Stay with the child.
- Explore for the trigger.
- Separate only if necessary.

If the child is already out of control or verging on it, it's up to the adult to supply the necessary control before even beginning to look for a cause of the anger. In the case of a child having a tantrum, we might remove the child from others or gain actual physical control over the child if harm could result. This could mean stopping a child from banging his head against something, restraining a child from hurting others by holding her, taking a child out of a public setting by picking him up, or, in the case of older children, setting strict limits on abusive language or threatening behavior, perhaps even removing oneself until things calm down. In extreme cases, if physical violence is a possibility, it may be necessary to call in outside help.

In the heat of the moment, it's sometimes hard to gauge just how serious or dangerous a situation is. This may be due to our own anxiety, feelings of helplessness, and anger. It's best to err on the side of safety, even if hindsight proves this an overreaction. We live and learn, after all, and that's something we can later explain to an angry child. In such an instance, the child may also learn what he did to provoke our overreaction.

Generally, the younger the child, the more action-oriented a caretaker must be. A preverbal youngster needs immediate and direct physical intervention. With a child who has a more developed vocabulary, it's possible to use words to help a child get control of herself.

The crucial thing to remember is that it's up to the parent to help a child gain some restraint before he causes damage to himself or others. This relieves the child's anxiety as well as minimizing the additional terror and anger that can come from feeling out of control. Sometimes intense anger feeds on itself. A child who's feeling helpless and angry and running amock into the bargain, is likely to experience only increasing helplessness and rage.

When a situation is somewhat less advanced and no real danger is involved, we might tell the child to get control of herself. We might suggest a time-out. Only then will we be able to help her. This sends a message about the constructive expression of angry feelings, as well as making a pitch for self-control. Our control helps the child feel under control.

When practicing anger first aid, we should try to stay with the child throughout the angry period.

There is an exception to this rule. Separate temporarily from the child if it will help to reduce the anger that's been triggered—if, for example, the child persists in seeing us as the cause. Rejoin the child as quickly as possible, as soon as you judge that the separation has had the desired effect of helping the child gain control.

Being present reassures the child that help will be forthcoming, and it also aids the parent in diagnosing the cause of the anger. A further benefit is that our presence lets the child know that anger doesn't frighten or repel us. It won't cause us to withdraw. Quite the opposite.

Wait until the severe anger episode has subsided and then try to explore for the trigger of the anger. Never do this during the storm of anger, but don't wait so long that the whole experience is forgotten, either.

Sometimes parents themselves may feel out of control because of helpless anger at a child. When that happens, an adult must separate from the child and get help from a third party until self-control returns.

Fortunately, most kids and parents don't have frequent episodes of anger that are completely out of control. When they do, the anger subsides quickly. Most of the time we can go right to locating the source of a child's distress, before it gets to this point.

## Locating the Source of the Child's Helpless Feelings

For the vast majority of everyday anger situations—and in the more uncommon ones in which anger needs first to be brought under control—a child's anger should be explored. Searching for a diagnosis of what caused the underlying feelings of helplessness in the first place is key.

A common parental error often occurs at this point. Many of us choose to become teachers or disciplinarians to the exclusion of being diagnosticians. There's a place for both roles, of course, but searching for the reason why our child is upset and then helping the child to understand it ought to come first. There's always time for a lecture about behavior or for meting out punishment, if necessary. Timing is what's important here. If we rush to judgment, punishment, or "education" and bypass the moment when we and our child can communicate about the anger, we've lost an opportunity.

*I once counseled a mother and son who'd had many joint therapy sessions. The boy hadn't, in fact, talked constructively to either of his parents for years. During the sessions with me he barely spoke at all, while his mother literally begged him to talk. Finally, one day he said he wanted to say something. When he began to talk, and his anger was obvious, his mother immediately admon-*

*ished him to keep quiet if he couldn't speak nicely
and without profanity. The look of despair the
young man gave me spoke volumes. He was locked
in an insoluble dilemma.*

This kind of judgmental parental response short-
circuits any further communication between parent
and child. Although the above case may seem extreme, it highlights a common problem. In angry interactions with their kids, parents sometimes tend to
pay more attention to the form of their child's message than to its content. The mother above could
have learned something about her son if she had listened to *what* he was saying rather than focusing on
*how* he was saying it. Disliking his style of expression, she launched into a lecture that effectively ren-
dered him mute once more.

## Observe, Listen, and Question

Assuming that we sidestep the pitfalls of immediately lecturing or disciplining an angry child, what's
the best way to discover why our child is angry? This
depends in part on the child's age. With preverbal
children, we have to play detective in a sense. Recall
those things discussed in Chapter Four that can induce helplessness in young children. Sift through
your knowledge of your own child. Try to make a
match between the two. In a way, this is similar to
the process pediatricians follow when they're treating infants. The patient can give little direct infor-

mation, so it's up to the doctor to use informed, deductive reasoning to figure out what's going on.

As children mature, a parent's mind keeps pace by constantly and automatically increasing its database, adding anything and everything our child does. Though probably unaware of it consciously, when parents are confronted with an angry child, they'll rapidly and automatically flip through these various files: Where has the child been? What has he been doing? What's been on his mind lately? What phase of development is he in? It's possible that this may shed some light on the cause of the anger.

In order to pinpoint the specific origin, it's likely that we'll need to observe our child patiently, listen intently to what she has to say, and ask some compassionate questions. One approach might be to raise the subject of anger ourselves, noting its connection with helplessness, and see what kind of reception we get. Another method is to wait for the child to come to us to let us know what's bothering her. However the discussion is initiated, the crucial message to convey to the child is that anger is understandable and that it's a sign of other underlying feelings. These may be fear, anxiety, or panic, all symptoms of a sense of helplessness. The way we explain this—in our own words, in whatever ways seems comfortable—will depend on the child's maturity and what she's able to understand.

Observe, listen, and question. Each of these is important. It is the compassionate questioning that's most valuable, and it often reveals the source of the difficulty and demonstrates caring.

It's often not effective to focus your questions directly on the anger itself, because this can come across as a veiled criticism of the child's angry feelings. When that happens, the child feels he's being judged and is more likely to clam up. Start with indirect and general questions, establishing rapport with your child, letting him know that you accept whatever he's feeling. The questions can grow more specific as you go along.

The following examples illustrate the benefits of indirect questioning:

> David, the six-year-old son of a friend of mine, was usually cheerful and curious, but when he and his dad came for a day's visit recently, he was cranky, irritable, and openly defiant to his father, Alex. David had been acting this way all weekend, Alex said, and it was probably because his wife was away visiting college friends. He'd asked David about this, but David said he wasn't mad and that he didn't care about his mother's going.
>
> Taking a more indirect approach, I began talking to David about his newly renovated bedroom. How did he spend his time in there? What toys did he have in it? What was it like to sleep in the new platform bed? Then I asked about his other activities in the house, about his family and the things they liked to do, and finally I zeroed in on

*the weekend. How was it to be spending it alone with his dad?*

*He didn't like it, David said. Because his mother was gone, there was too much work to do around the house. Also, his dad wasn't a very good cook and David didn't like the food they'd been having. Then he turned to his father and asked when his mother would be coming home. During the course of this discussion, David's anger abated.*

*When I asked Alex later why he hadn't explored all this with David, he said that he'd thought bringing it up would just make David feel worse about the separation from his mother. He also admitted that he was himself angry at his wife for going off for the weekend.*

*Nancy was four, her parents were divorced, and each time she returned from a visit to her father, she cried inconsolably for at least an hour, couldn't sleep that night, and was unable to go to school the next day. She also acted outraged with her mother, yelling at her for everything she did. Nancy's mother asked the father about it, but he said he had no idea why their daughter would act that way. When her mother asked Nancy what was upsetting her, she'd simply heap more blame on her mother. When she'd ask if anything upsetting happened over the weekend, Nancy said no.*

*Realizing she was getting nowhere, Nancy's mother shifted gears and began to ask general questions about the weekend: how Nancy spent her time, what she did with her father, and so on. It became apparent that Nancy's father paid very little attention to her when she visited. Soon after she'd arrive, in fact, he and his new girlfriend would go out to dinner, leaving Nancy with a babysitter. When her father ran errands during the weekend, he'd leave Nancy home. Nancy, feeling unwanted and unloved by her father, was enraged at him, but afraid to let him know this for fear of further alienating him. Instead, she directed her anger at her mother.*

In both these cases, head-on exploration of the child's anger wasn't productive, but indirect questioning yielded results. This is especially true for younger children, although it can be useful for teenagers and even adults. The very process of this compassionate questioning is important. Both David's and Nancy's anger diminished during it. This happened because someone was paying sympathetic attention to them and their distress.

Think how differently things might have gone if the emphasis had been placed, for instance, on behavior control ("I've had enough of that crying!") or admonitions ("I don't want to see you again until there's a smile on your face"), or punishments ("If that's how you're going to behave, you may spend the weekend in your room"). Any of these would have ended the opportunity for communication. The parent would have remained in the dark about why the child was angry; the child's distress wouldn't have lessened. However, a gentle, probing investigation of the child's feelings led to discovery of the anger's origins and made both parent and child feel better.

I can imagine parents reading this and muttering to themselves: "Easy for him to say, but he's not standing there in the living room with so-and-so when she's screaming at the top of her lungs." Perhaps the steps I've suggested seem a bit idealized and simplistic when placed next to the picture of a raging, belligerent, offensive, out-of-control youngster, but they work, and they lead to the constructive handling of anger if parents will stick with them consistently.

Remember these basic premises:

- See your child's anger as a signal of distress.
- Control potentially destructive anger by nonharmful methods, staying with the child physically whenever possible.
- Remember that the primary goal is to help relieve the child's sense of helplessness.
- Gather information about why your child feels helpless. Often the most effective way to do this is by indirect, compassionate questioning—minus judgment and/or punishment—observation, and sensitive listening.

## Taking Action

Once the cause of a child's anger is revealed, what should we do about it?

In many cases, as I've said, simply accepting your child's anger and helping to discover its cause may bring great relief. Often, further strategies are necessary as well to reduce our child's anger.

In general, the younger the child is, the more directly parents will need to intervene when the child's feeling distressed. Extremely young children can't change the thermostat, undo the blanket that's become twisted around them, or take a second helping of food. All of those things are responsibilities of the parents.

Of course, as children start to mature, parents can begin to back off. You don't want to rob your children of the chance to try out their own ways of dealing with obstacles that they come up against. These opportunities are crucial steps in their growth and they foster self-confidence and children's ability to operate on their own.

Sometimes, beyond infancy, situations arise in our youngsters' lives that do require parental intervention. There's a point where avoiding this becomes harmful to your child. If intervention is necessary, parents must decide what form it should take. When deciding, always remember that your job as a parent is to try to alleviate your child's sense of helplessness. The levels of intervention range from support with a minimum of hands-on intrusion to direct interference in the anger-producing environment. Interventions include:

- Supporting Mastery
- Suggesting solutions for repetitive problems
- Giving direct assistance
- Direct intervention in the environment
- Working on ourselves

*Support the child's own feeling of mastery.* This might involve helping an angry toddler to get up and try walking again; bolstering a rejected teenager by recounting one's own painful adolescent love life and encouraging attendance at a dance even though someone else will be dancing with an ex; or anticipating a developmental step, such as acquiring language, and helping a youngster prepare by supplying new words; or helping a school-ager get used to being in school all day by noting and being interested in how he accomplishes a project.

*Three-year-old Eileen never liked sharing her toys when other youngsters visited. Her mother helped her with this by pointing out how good it made her friends feel when Eileen shared with them. She also reminded her daughter how good she felt when a friend shared something special with her.*

*Mary, who had many junior high friends who
called her daily, became regularly angry because
she got few calls from a particular clique of girls.
Her parents pointed out that she'd chosen her true
friends based on characteristics that she really
liked, a good quality. Her concern with getting
attention from the excluding clique, on the other
hand, was based on rather superficial reasons.
Her parents' approach confirmed Mary's basic
good judgment and helped her to shift her focus
back to the solid friendships that she'd established.*

*Nine-year-old Freddy, on the other hand, be-
came more frustrated each day with his inability
to write a report assigned in school. This was evident in his increasingly foul language and his
outbursts of rage. Suggesting that the two of them
go to the library, Freddy's father showed his son
where to find the encyclopedias and other refer-
ence books and also introduced him to some general principles of research. Freddy ended up
having fun, and in the process his feelings of
competence and self-sufficiency grew. By dinner-
time, his anger was gone.*

At this level of intervention, the parent smoothes
a child's way by a small but important boost. It
doesn't involve pushing the child but, rather, supple-

menting normal developmental progression or applauding a neophyte's job.

**Suggest solutions to recurrent problems.** Sometimes kids seem stuck in repetitive, anger-inducing ruts, and these patterns seem to stall a child's development. While obvious to parents, kids may be completely unaware of patterns that continually produce frustration and anger. In such cases, it's a parent's responsibility to help get a child back on track, rather than allowing her to continue spinning her wheels. Parents need to alert kids to such patterns by, for example, noting a child's repeated efforts to succeed at an athletic level that's simply beyond her capacity, simultaneously suggesting other activities; or pointing out how a floundering school-age child's self-defeating study habits lead to repeated failure at homework assignments.

*Bobby always got irritable in the days before an assignment was due in his fourth grade class, but he'd let everything go until the deadline was upon him. Recognizing that he grew panicky and angry because he couldn't manage to plan ahead, his mother suggested and helped to establish a schedule for him to follow. This was instrumental in breaking Bobby's anger-producing pattern.*

*Suzie regularly invited Harold to come over, even though he never accepted. Her mother said she certainly understood Suzie's anger, but sug-*

*gested that it might be resolved if her daughter could find out why Harold kept saying no. Suzie set her mind to the task and discovered that Harold's shyness was the reason. Suzie felt less rejected and, consequently, less angry.*

***Give direct assistance.*** Sometimes, no amount of bolstering, praise, or suggestions can aid an angry child. We all know that infants frequently need direct assistance but, as kids get older, the issue isn't so clear-cut. Are we being overbearing or helpful when we step into angry situations involving our children? Are we undermining their ability to develop their own coping skills? On the other hand, does a laissez-faire approach simply prolong their agony? The best rule of thumb is this: If the first two levels of intervention fail to ease your child's distress, then take direct action.

*Each time thirteen-year-old Amanda hit the tennis ball, it went into the net and she lost her temper. It made no difference that her father was watching and instructing from the sidelines. When he joined her on the court and showed her the correct grip and the right form and follow-through, it made an immediate difference.*

*Arnold couldn't get the hang of riding his new two-wheeler. Each time he pushed off from the curb, he fell and grew more furious. His uncle, who was watching, realized that the seven-year-*

*old wasn't coordinating the pedals correctly. When he showed his nephew how to do it, after several tries Arnold had it down pat. No more falls; no more rage.*

*Four-year-old Suzanne wanted desperately to be friendly with Max, her neighbor's cocker spaniel, but her overtures consisted of running up behind him and pulling his tail. The dog, of course, ran away each time and Suzanne collapsed in rageful tears. Things changed, however, when the little girl's father taught her to approach a dog from the front and to pet him gently.*

*Jack was nine, but his inability to tread water kept him stuck in the beginners' swimming class at day camp long after his peers had moved on. He took his anger out on the other campers, frequently picking fights. His instructor, however, had his hands full with a large class and couldn't give Jack special attention. One weekend, his older cousin took him to a pool and taught him how to stay afloat, in more ways than one, and the rest of Jack's summer was much happier.*

Sometimes children are just too angry to respond to a small boost or a helpful suggestion, and direct assistance is necessary. This isn't cheating. It's only harmful when a child automatically turns to a caretaker for assistance in many different situations, becoming passive in the process.

*Direct intervention in the environment.*
There are times when, no matter how we try to help,
a child can't overcome the factors in his environment
that are causing intense feelings of helplessness and
anger. If we decide this is the case, it's mandatory
that we step in and attempt to change the situation.
The thorny question at this level of intervention is
whether or not a child is accurately reporting the
situation. Is she the victim of unjust prejudice on a
teacher's part? Is the coach really unfair? Do other
children treat him badly without provocation? Are
other parents arbitrarily forbidding their child to so-
cialize with ours?

Unless your child habitually blames others for
everything that goes wrong, give her the benefit of
the doubt. Assume she's reporting her situation accurately. It's better to err on that side of the issue
and to investigate your child's complaint than to let
it fall on deaf ears. Generally, youngsters respond
well to discussing how they may contribute to a
problem and are able to take some responsibility for
angry entanglements.

*Charlie, who was behind the other fifth graders
in his class in all his subjects, was very down on
himself. In fact, he'd taken to calling himself "stupid," harping on his mistakes, even carrying his
shoulders in a constant slump of defeat. When his
parents learned that his inexperienced teacher
was unable to focus on constructive measures,*

*they asked the principal to get special remediation, including help with a reading disability, for Charlie's academic weaknesses. He improved rapidly and soon looked and sounded more like his old self.*

*Every day Mary, who was nine, complained about her classmate Samantha, who was a head taller, a big tease, and a bully in the cloak room. Mary's parents gave her some self-defense tips, but Sammy continued pushing her around and enlisted others in what began to feel like a witch-hunt, humiliating Mary publicly. Finally, Mary's parents insisted on a meeting with Sammy's parents, arranged by the school guidance counselor. Fortunately, Sammy's parents weren't overly defensive and they successfully managed to get their daughter to back off.*

*Returning in tears from her piano lesson, Louise made disparaging remarks about her own playing and then reported that her teacher criticized her continually for not being "the best." "She always yells at me," complained the eight-year-old. Her parents talked to the teacher and discovered her to be a stubborn perfectionist, a trait they'd missed upon their first meeting. Louise began enjoying her musical talents when she changed teachers.*

These youngsters were caught in situations where they felt helpless due to a fixed factor in their environment, and only a change in environment could alleviate their anger. Direct parental intervention was necessary to effect the change.

Situations aren't always as clear-cut as the examples I've given to illustrate the four levels of intervention parents may consider when their child is angry, but don't worry about taking an action when things are somewhat murkier. The important thing is to offer help and to remember that this can range from gentle support to eliminating environmental pressures. What's helpful will vary with a child's age and situation. Parents need to remain flexible and view each angry occurrence on its own terms.

## When We Are the Source of Distress

Parents also need to be aware of another set of circumstances that makes helping an angry child particularly difficult. That's when we, ourselves, are part of the problem, when we are causing the child's anger.

This is common. Of course we love our children, and of course we're basically good and caring, but we're also human beings, with all the failings that implies, and parenthood doesn't confer on us automatic wisdom and foolproof conduct. How many of us have caught ourselves in the anger-inducing behaviors I spoke of in Chapter Five?

We're sometimes unaware of the part we play in our child's anger problem, or perhaps we're unwilling to acknowledge it. It's not easy to own up to the fact that we may be overprotective, neglectful, harshly punitive, or so inconsistent that we send our kids confusing, damaging double messages. It takes courage to face such things in ourselves. Don't confuse this with self-indulgent guilt that involves our assuming responsibility for absolutely everything that happens to our children and that paradoxically blinds us from any really clear vision of our own responsibilities.

When we're tracking down the reasons why our kids are mad, let's be willing to begin by looking in the mirror. We need to examine our own behavior, to ask ourselves the difficult questions. If we discover that, knowingly or unknowingly, we've been a part of the problem, we need to own up to it, apologize to our child if it's appropriate and, most importantly, make the effort to change.

Of course, this isn't easy, but it's well worth the effort. Beyond simply dealing with our child's anger, it has a beneficial side effect, which is no small thing in itself. We can set a powerful example for our child by admitting to a fault and attempting to change it. When we do, it's well to remember that there's no need to wallow in destructive self-criticism. Just act appropriately and this will, indeed, speak louder than any words.

## Helping with the Big Questions

Sometimes, in order to help our children with anger, we have to become philosophers of a sort, offering wisdom about certain life issues. Life inevitably presents all of us with painful situations—loss, separation, death, and other universal phenomena. Sooner or later, nearly everyone faces certain difficult psychological facts of life such as the likelihood of failure, the recognition of our own limitations, the inevitability of disappointment. All of these things gradually enter children's lives as they mature; all of them induce feelings of helplessness.

Kids don't automatically understand these difficult matters. Think of how troublesome they can be to us even as adults. It's up to us, as parents, to help our children as they struggle to absorb and adjust to these aspects of life. The way we explain to a five-year-old the death of the beloved family cat will be quite different from how we discuss an impending marital separation with a teenager. Telling a three-year-old that Mom and Dad are going away for a week isn't the same as revealing to a preteen that the family has to relocate because of a job change. Whatever our child's age, don't think of these as simply matters to be announced or information to be imparted and let it go at that. In ways that are appropriate to our child's needs at a given time, it's up to us to address these issues and the feelings that they raise in our kids.

Children have no control over any of the above circumstances. They're bound to feel a sense of helplessness as they face such major losses or separations, and anger, as we know, will accompany the helplessness. We can help them to handle this anger.

*Eight-year-old John's grandfather died after a long illness for which he'd been hospitalized many times. Whenever he'd gone back into the hospital, there'd been a new treatment prescribed, and each time, John would become cranky and somewhat disobedient and withdraw socially. When the grandfather finally died, John's mother realized that not only was her son experiencing loss, but that he'd also been exposed to the raised expectations of each new treatment and felt angry when each failed and the illness recurred.*

*She explained to John that sometimes we hope for things that we don't get and that it's natural to be disappointed. He got angry, John's mother explained, because he'd been sure each time that the new treatment would help; but instead, it had failed. John couldn't have learned these lessons, she told him, without these experiences.*

*When twelve-year-old Marissa lost in the qualifying round of her school's hundred-yard-dash event, she was quite angry. She'd been practicing for two months, while the girl who won hadn't even worked out once. She was just naturally a faster runner. Marissa learned early in life a hard lesson for all of us: In some areas, no matter how hard we try, other people will simply do better, possess more innate talent, or have better instincts. Her parents helped Marissa to accept her limitations as a runner by discussing her anger and by showing her the positive things she'd gained by making a commitment to reach a goal she'd set.*

When it comes to introducing our children to life's hard knocks and thorny issues or helping them to accept them, what we say isn't the only important thing. All the wise words we can muster may not carry as much weight as how our own kids see us behave when we're facing tough times. If they watch us adjusting to the inevitably painful and difficult aspects of life that make us feel helpless and angry, it will strengthen them and help them to tolerate adversity in their own lives.

Remember, when handling our children's anger:

- Practice anger first aid if things seem out of control.
- Locate the source of distress by observation, listening, and compassionate questions, not by lecturing.
- Take action to reduce anger by supporting the mastering of a situation, giving suggestions for repetitive dilemmas, offering direct assistance, and by looking to see if you are the cause of the anger.

# CHAPTER SEVEN

# Special Situations

Developmental hurdles and everyday stresses cause anger on a regular, almost predictable, basis. There are also some common complex situations that are almost guaranteed to be associated with important anger issues. These situations—third-party child care, divorce, illness, attention deficit disorder, separation and loss, and sexual abuse—deserve specific attention.

## CHILD CARE

Caretakers other than parents have become regular fixtures in our culture during recent years. Larger numbers of women have entered the workforce, single parent families have increased, and even two-parent families find it harder to get by economically on just one salary. These child care helpers, with whom many of us leave our children for at least some part of each day, include nannies, housekeepers, workers in day care centers, babysitters, au pairs, willing relatives, special instructors or coaches, and even neighbors.

As the need for and number of third-party caretakers has increased, we've also been exposed to dramatic and widely publicized accounts of abuses by this group. Sometimes these abuses have proven to be real, sometimes not. When the latter is true, we don't hear as much about it as we did about the original charges. No data indicate that child abuse of any sort is more likely to be committed by child care helpers than by the population as a whole.

Of course, anger issues do arise with third-party caretakers. Just as with parents, the most important issue is how they handle the anger of the children in their charge. Sometimes child care workers come from backgrounds and cultures that treat anger very differently from the way a particular child's parents do. Sometimes neighbors with whom we have much in common or even members of our own families have attitudes about anger that differ radically from ours.

When children are exposed to these inconsistencies, they may feel confused and frustrated, and they may become angry as a result. So it's important to choose a third-party caretaker with this in mind. This can be accomplished in a relaxed, detailed interview during which a parent can assess a prospective helper's attitudes toward anger. Give detailed examples of potentially angry situations and ask how she'd deal with them. At the very least, parents and the caretaker ought to agree on a general approach to handling kids' angry feelings and behaviors.

Another issue is how a child expresses anger toward the caretaker. Ideally, children should see the child care helper as a stand-in for the parents, with equal authority and shared values. Many youngsters, unfortunately, act as though it's their right to behave toward their caretakers however they like. This includes expressing anger in ways they wouldn't consider trying out on their parents. At the same time, the caretaker may tend to suffer such treatment silently, bending over backward not to alienate the child, fearing she'll jeopardize her position. This isn't a constructive situation for anyone involved, and it's one that parents need to be on the alert for.

It's also true, of course, that child care helpers may harbor negative feelings toward their charges and the children's parents. This may have nothing to do with a child's behavior. If these caretakers are working in a family's home, they most likely come from less affluent backgrounds, which may cause them to feel resentful, envious, and even spiteful. It's possible that they may act out these feelings toward the children. Again, parental awareness and alertness is important.

Parents need to be equally aware of the strong bond that children may form with these people who help to care for them. In some instances, youngsters spend more time with the third-party caretaker than they do with their parents, and they may receive from her a great deal of loving attention and concern. When life circumstances such as a visa expiration or financial considerations cause this bond to be interrupted, a child is bound to feel distressed and angry. Although parents may think little about replacing one caretaker with another, repeated separations from caretakers are very hard on kids.

Often, parents feel unnecessarily guilty for having to hire a caretaker or for placing their child in a day care situation in the first place. This guilt may trigger behavior in parents that makes a child very angry. A parent, for example, may be overly critical of a caretaker, whom the child loves. The parent may imagine the child has begun to prefer the caretaker to her, and feel jealous. This could lead to the caretaker's dismissal or to the parent granting the child anything, refusing to set any limits, in order to win back the affection she feels she's lost. Neither of these outcomes is good for the child.

When selecting a child care worker:

- Don't be afraid to ask any questions you want about background, mental illness, or criminal records.
- Speak at length with references for whom the person has worked.
- Ask specific questions about anger, discipline, and the person's own childhood anger atmosphere.
- Prepare the worker for your particular child's temperament and unique ways of expressing anger.
- Prepare the child to see the caretaker as an authoritative stand-in for you.

• Never underestimate the constructive and strong bond that can develop between your child and the caretaker. Treat it with respect, not jealousy. The child always knows who his parent is.

## DIVORCE

We hear so much about divorce today—through the media, special education programs at schools, and from friends—that we practically take it for granted. It's become so commonplace in our culture that some of us have been fooled into thinking that it's run-of-the-mill even for the children whose lives it touches. Nothing could be farther from the truth.

Anyone involved in a divorce finds it traumatic. For children, who are the most vulnerable to the complicated emotions it arouses, the trauma is often severe.

Generally, before two parents actually separate and one leaves the home, there have been years of problems between them. Some of these are easy to spot, as they're out in the open, such as arguing, constant conflict, and even violence. Others are reflected in coldness between the parents, a sense of alienation, or even indifference; they may be living under the same roof but have little to do with one another.

No matter how the problems display themselves, children seldom miss any of them. Sensing or knowing that their parents are having trouble is threatening. Kids worry about losing one parent or the other and about what will happen to them if their parents split up. This frightens children and makes the foundations of their lives feel extremely shaky.

Also, children frequently feel guilty and responsible for their parents' obvious difficulties. Partly, this is because they're immature and egocentric; they feel that everything in life revolves around them. More importantly, when parents wrangle, often the child's own name comes up and he concludes that he must be the cause of the fights.

The children may become victims of the angry feelings that a parent really wants to direct at his or her partner. The anger spills over or gets displaced onto the children. In these instances, kids start to feel that maybe if they changed their behavior—if they weren't so "bad," if they got better grades, if they made fewer demands, if they were prettier, stronger, or didn't cry so easily—their parents would get along better. In other words, they start to feel responsible for their parents' problems. These are some of the feelings that begin to build up in children before divorce even occurs.

We've already seen that normal growth and development can be tumultuous for youngsters. Kids get angry and frustrated under the best conditions. Consider how much more difficult growing up becomes when children are living in an atmosphere of constant tension and turmoil between their parents.

When the actual separation occurs, all of the child's previous fears and feelings are heightened, with some new ones added. They fear that they'll be abandoned; they feel rejected by one parent or both; they feel grief and loss; and they feel more guilt and anger.

Of course, a child's age is a factor in how he or she responds, but even for very young children the experience of divorce can produce evident signs of anger and distress. Toddlers and preschoolers might show this in developmental regression in their motor or language skills, or they might throw tantrums, become weepy, withdraw, or cling to a parent tenaciously. School age children could begin having academic difficulties. Teenagers might exhibit a variety of angry symptoms, such as mood disorders, substance abuse, or overtly rebellious behavior. All of these behaviors, as discussed previously, signal a child's underlying sense of helplessness.

After all what can they do to change the course of events? They're faced with what feels like the collapse of their lives, and they're powerless to prevent it. This sense of impotence, combined with feelings of great loss and fear, produce enormous anger in a child.

The other adjustments divorce necessitates may cause even more anger for youngsters. Economic circumstances may change, and usually not for the better. The noncustodial parent is no longer regularly available. There may be a geographic move and, consequently, the necessity of getting used to a new school and making new friends. Continuing conflict between the parents may cause children to feel they have to take sides; their loyalties are torn between two people they love. A child can easily become a scapegoat in divorce situations, as parents take out their own frustrations on a son or daughter. Quite suddenly, children's parents have new friends, go on dates, or become involved in love relationships with other partners; some of these people may have families of their own, yet another hurdle.

Unfortunately, of course, at the very moment when parents' support and help is crucial, they may be so distracted and drained by their own concerns that they don't give their children what they need. Many people going through divorce experience emotional problems, and while they're grappling with these, they may not do such great jobs as parents. Just as kids are forced into circumstances that are bound to produce great anger, those same circumstances make it more likely that their anger will be mishandled, and the situation can last for years.

In the wake of a divorce, parents may mishandle their child's anger by neglecting it due to their own depression and withdrawal. They may stimulate anger further by continually playing off each other through the child, putting her right in the middle of their conflicts. Due to guilt about the divorce, they may try to crush their children's anger since it's a nasty reminder that they don't want to see or hear about. Unconsciously identifying with the child's anger may make a parent want to squelch it as well. Sometimes the parents' guilt may make them over-solicitous and fearful of putting any controls on the child's anger; this, as we know, does the child no favor, either.

Even one of these situations would be difficult enough for a child, and sometimes children are faced with many or all of them. It is a lot to ask young people to handle, and we mustn't fall into the trap of thinking that they can do just fine without our help. Parents must stay aware of the pitfalls and take great pains to help a child deal with divorce-induced anger. Otherwise, the likelihood is that these kids will develop one of the legacies of mishandled anger, which is discussed in Chapter Eight.

Here are some constructive steps to take if you are in the midst of separation or divorce:

- Keep children out of the conflicts. Discussions should be accurate, and children should not be used as messengers.
- Reassure children that they're not responsible for their parents' problems.
- Continue to focus on the child's needs after the separation/divorce.
- Alert children in advance of impending lifestyle changes, let them know specifically what to expect, and join in helping them deal with the stress of change constructively.

- Talk openly about children's fears, resentments, and anger and never force them—overtly or covertly—to take sides.
- When possible, focus on the constructive aspects of the situation. Some problems that have existed won't be an issue anymore. More time will be suitable to be with the child now that problems will be resolved. Let them know that other people have successfully navigated these waters.
- If you feel unable to furnish these kinds of support for your children, get professional help to strengthen you.

## ILLNESS

Stressful for anyone, illness in children can arouse a wide range of thoughts and feelings in them. One of these is worry about their symptoms and the fear of getting sicker. They may also feel guilt and believe that they've somehow caused their illness by being bad. Children frequently suffer great anxiety over the things that go along with treating their illness: being stuck with needles, confronted by a string of doctors, or having their bodies exposed or harmed in some way.

Kids feel scared, even panicky, when they're sick, and we know that a sense of fright and helplessness causes anger. There's nothing abnormal about this. Parental awareness—and healthy handling of predictable anger—can go a long way toward relieving the fears of a sick child. Children who get this kind of appropriate care won't be emotionally scarred by illness, no matter what emotions they go through during it.

When a child has a chronic or long-lasting illness, the stresses are even greater, harder to relieve, and produce a lot more anger. First of all, a chronic condition sets the child apart from normal kids. When a child feels different from other youngsters his age, he may experience feelings of inferiority and alienation. If chronic illness exists, the disease itself produces further stresses such as the possibility that it may cause death, continual pain, limits on normal activities, having no control over what's happening, constant monitoring of body functions, bouts of relapse, and the need for medication or special care.

Chronic illness provokes lots of different reactions even from loving and concerned caretakers; some of these may create still more stress. Who wouldn't be mad in a situation carrying this amount of freight? Who wouldn't resent even a few of these factors?

Chronically ill children may feel that their parents somehow caused the illness and be angry about that, or about their parents' inability to cure them. They may be mad at the doctors taking care of them; after all, treatment sometimes causes discomfort; and they may be mad at themselves, imagining that they have caused the illness by misbehaving or by harboring hostile thoughts and feelings toward others. They may, in effect, see their illness as a punishment.

What about the parents of children who are chron-

ically ill? The tragedy of having such a child is difficult for every mother and father. No one handles it
perfectly. However, the parents' attitudes have an
enormous effect on how a sick child adjusts to illness and may even play a part in the physical out-
come as well.

Parents' reactions to a child's illness are as different as their personalities, of course, just as with anything else, but there are also some patterns that
many parents share. Understandably, varying de-
grees of overprotective behavior is one of the most
common. We've seen repeatedly how damaging this
can be, as it interferes with a child's independence
and development. It's important to remember that
establishing independence and enjoying unham-
pered development within the limitations dictated by
their illness are just as important to sick children as
they are to well ones. When these desires are
thwarted, rebellion is common.

*A ten-year-old boy had a very mild heart mur-
mur and terrified and hovering parents. Years
earlier, after he'd become short of breath during
a bout of overexertion, they'd clamped severe re-
strictions on his activities despite a pediatrician's directive that their son could handle more
leeway. The parents, however, were frightened
when he exerted himself at all, and ruled out any
sort of athletics as impossible. This made him so
mad that he battled them continually at home,
misbehaved in school and, most interestingly,*

*jogged and rode his bike at great length which did bring on mild breathing difficulties. Perhaps if his parents had given him more slack, along with sensibly monitoring the effects of mild exercise, his rebellion wouldn't have been necessary.*

*Some years ago, I met a twelve-year-old daredevil who was referred to me because he'd climbed a 200-foot-high building, gotten stuck on top during an electrical storm, and nearly fallen off in a panic. Finally, fire and police crews had to rescue him.*

*This kind of foolhardy behavior had started when he was six and was diagnosed with mild allergic asthma. His mother, whose father had recently died from chronic emphysema, which is similar to asthma in some ways, reacted to her son's condition with a smothering preoccupation. She was constantly on the lookout for allergic signs, took him to get shots, installed oxygen tanks in the house, made him practice giving himself epinephrine injections, and was terrified by the slightest sniffle or wheeze. Her handsome, graceful, athletic son responded to this massive overreaction with rage that took the form of extremely reckless behavior.*

Of course, overprotection isn't the only parental response that causes anger in a chronically ill child. Because of unconscious guilt about a child's condition, some parents adopt rejecting attitudes, shunning the ill child, which certainly induces anger in that child. Some may react to a child's illness with overt anger, perhaps even victimizing the ill child with physical abuse. Still other parents may try to deny their child's illness by pushing him or her to overachieve in unrealistic ways, given the child's disabilities. Then they applaud their child's bravado. Sometimes children's illnesses make parents so anxious that they act ambivalently and inconsistently, creating confusion and great anger in their children.

The following general strategies can help a parent constructively handle the stress and anger resulting from a child's illness.

If your child suffers a reversible acute illnesses such as fever, sore throat, an intestinal malady, etc.:

- Gather the correct information about the illness such as its duration and treatment procedures.
- Reassure the child about the passing nature of the disorder.
- Outline the treatment with the child.
- Always listen to the child's fears.

If your child must undergo surgery:

- Take advantage of the surgery preparations offered by nearly all pediatric surgery departments. This will help your child understand the procedures to be done, and develop feelings of mastery and optimism. These preparations are given by trained professionals, and often include the parents.

If your child has a chronic illness:

- Get all information possible about the course of the illness, including constructive estimates of the possible future development and degree of disability incurred by the disease.
- Continually bolster your child's sense of confidence by supporting and stressing areas of competence.
- Always listen to your child's grief about the condition.

With all ill children:

- Be alert to your own signs of distress, which commonly include impatience, hopelessness, guilt, anger, self-pity, and resignation.
- Discuss these feelings with other family members or friends, or consult a professional if you can't seem to get a handle on them and feel they're impinging on your sick child.
- No matter how upsetting for a parent, don't cut off your child's communications of pain, helplessness, fear, rage, and panic.
- Parent support groups are very helpful, not only in stressing what everyone has in common, but also in teaching techniques for dealing with shared difficulties.

## ATTENTION DEFICIT DISORDER

Over the years, this common neurological childhood disorder has been called many things. Minimal brain damage, minimal brain dysfunction, and hyperactive child syndrome are some of them. Whatever the label, youngsters with this problem are vulnerable to developing great anger and to having their anger mishandled. Because they're impulsive, have trouble paying attention, and often find it hard to maintain normal patterns of activity, others are liable to get very mad at them, which isn't hard to understand. In school, they can't focus on what's in front of them, they seem not to listen, they don't finish assignments, and their work is often sloppy and careless.

As if these problems weren't hard enough for a teacher, many of these kids are never able to be still. They pop in and out of their seats, fidget, and always have some part of themselves in motion. They're often impatient, find it hard to wait their turn, and frequently interrupt others. Their motors seem to race all the time as they jump from one activity to another, causing chaos and trouble wherever they go. They're the bulls in the china shop, making a mess of things, literally and figuratively. It's as though they ride emotional roller coasters, with their moods swinging between extremes. Their social judgment is often poor, too, and that gets them into even more trouble.

Also, these children very often have learning disabilities. Combined with their disruptive presences and poor judgment, they develop reputations as troubled or even mentally retarded kids. In fact, their intelligence, which is usually normal, is seldom the problem.

Obviously, it's not unusual for such children to be rejected and criticized. In order to protect themselves from feeling like passive victims, they often adopt the role of class clown or tough guy. Doing this enables them to gain some feeling of control.

At present, it's assumed that this disorder involves impaired functioning of the child's central nervous system, though other factors such as severe early psychosocial deprivation, physical abuse, and an overall deficient environment may contribute to the problem in some children.

Whatever its origin, it's understandable that children with this disorder develop a large store of anger at themselves and others, and when they're angry, they have a hard time controlling it, exploding the moment they feel frustrated, throwing temper tantrums, and giving free rein to provocative behavior. Given their failures, the abuse they often suffer, and the ridicule directed at them, these kids don't feel very good about themselves. As understandable as their anger is, so is that of the adults dealing with them. They deserve sympathy as well.

If parents can attune themselves to a child with

A.D.D., however, it can help to avert the legacies of mishandled anger. Coming to understand the various, often subtle psychological problems these children have communicating, learning, and controlling themselves and dealing with their distress is most helpful.

Youngsters with this disorder are a handful and are likely to cause enormous frustration in others. This, of course, increases the risk that when these kids get mad, their anger will be mishandled. A parent who feels pestered to the limit has a hard time responding constructively.

These children are often treated quite badly, which leads to increased anger on their part, an anger metamorphosis, and development of one of the legacies of mishandled anger. The legacies I've seen most often in such kids are further aggressive disorders, depression, substance abuse and, predictably, chronic school failure.

This bleak picture can be averted however if the disorder is recognized and properly treated. Proper diagnosis, usually by a child psychiatrist, is crucial. Help consists of a multidisciplinarian approach that includes the teacher, remediation specialists, behavioral or psychotherapeutic intervention, and sometimes medication.

When treated humanely and with understanding, they needn't be doomed to a legacy of buried anger. Children with A.D.D. cannot only adjust to their disabilities but overcome them. Many successful adults have conquered this disability because of the compassionate care they received as children.

## SEPARATION AND LOSS

The distress children feel when separation occurs can have many meanings. Forced to part from an adult—no matter who's going away, parent or child—may cause a child to feel abandoned, punished, or frightened by a sense of having to fend for herself. The child's age and circumstances make a difference in how she experiences and expresses this distress. Parents should keep in mind that the anger accompanying separation isn't just a distress signal. It often represents an effort to change the painful situation as well, and it sometimes even serves as a child's avenue of revenge.

For example, a toddler who begins to squall when she sees her parents dressing to go out for the evening is not only expressing distress-induced anger at the departure, she's also hoping that the anger will keep her parents from going. This is true for separations that range from something as simple as a child briefly parting from a parent or going to sleep at night, to a school age child going away to summer camp, having parents leave on a vacation, or to the most complex separation, death itself.

Anger goes hand-in-hand with grief over the loss of someone we love. When children are dealing with someone's death, it's especially important not to mishandle their anger. His anger is very hard for a child to bear because he often feels guilty about it as well. How can he be so horrid as to feel angry at his dying mother? He must be an awful person to be mad at his beloved grandfather at the end of his life.

It's important to remember that the anger that goes along with grief is very complex, as is any separation anger. It is a message of distress, a wish to reverse the situation, and sometimes a tool of revenge against the important person who's causing the distress. All of these are natural phenomena.

Studies show that frequent separations occurring in early childhood or the use of separation threats as punishments produce some of the most destructive anger in children. The younger a child is, the greater his or her psychological fragility. In many psychiatric syndromes that are particularly hard to treat, one can look back to early life and find at the core of the cause serious separation and loss issues and mishandling of the anger they induced.

The following suggestions will help your child cope with separation and loss:

- Prepare a child for separations such as sleep, school, camp, or even college to bolster a sense of confidence and decrease distress.
- Rehearsals, storytelling, gradual transitions, and similar techniques all help children to feel they can handle what lies ahead. These also help, when pos-

sible, with the impending loss of a loved one.
- Parents must try to be open to a child's angry communications.

## CHILD SEXUAL ABUSE

Like children who are subjected to physical abuse, victims of sexual abuse develop great anger. Because the sexual abuser tends to act chronically and repetitively, there is little relief from the anger. Children who are subject to this extreme and powerful violation develop a great reservoir of helpless, angry feelings, which are usually buried and repressed. Sooner or later, this anger is expressed by one or more of the legacies, most commonly in a cluster of symptoms.

Like victims of physical abuse, the symptoms a sexually abused youngster displays could be caused by other things as well. There is no single sign, no one legacy, that points to certain sexual abuse. While uncovering sexual abuse most often takes a careful, thorough diagnostic assessment, the list below offers possible tip-offs to a sexually abusive situation, especially if several appear in a given child.

- Secrecy
- High anxiety, phobias, sleep disturbances
- Withdrawn behavior
- Angry outbursts, tantrums, explosiveness
- Guilt

- Depression or flat mood
- Recall of the abuse through anxiety-producing flashbacks that a child reports to adults
- Sexually inappropriate behavior such as teenage promiscuity or precocious sexuality, even in very young children
- Substance abuse
- Suicide attempts and other impulsive behavior

Child sexual abuse, along with physical abuse and neglect, has received increasing attention in recent years. There are many places to go for help with this difficult and shattering problem. Many areas have a hot line to offer advice and referrals, parent and child support groups also offer assistance, and many therapists specialize in helping people deal with issues raised by sexual and physical abuse.

Remember, being sexually abused causes a child to feel utterly alone and powerless. These children need careful, sympathetic, and often prolonged help in overcoming this type trauma.

## SIBLINGS

Until recently, the words "sibling" and "rivalry" have been inextricably linked. Especially in a book about anger, one would expect to see the relationship between brothers and sisters treated exclusively as a source of corrosive anger in the family. However, there can be much more to siblings' relations than jockeying for position, and the rivalry that may exist isn't necessarily bad.

Siblings assist each other in many ways. One may serve as a role model for another, a caretaker, a conduit for information about social customs and other matters, or simply as a friendly, helping hand. In the face of stress in the family, siblings often band together as companions and give each other comfort. I've found in many of my patients that siblings were the primary healthy force in their lives when their parents were having trouble.

Of course siblings compete or act occasionally as rivals, but there's nothing wrong with that in and of itself. One sibling, for instance, may set the pace for developing a certain trait or skill. Another may strive to meet it and improve in the bargain, widen her interests, or try something she might otherwise have avoided. This is simply good role modeling. Competing with a sibling also introduces children to what they'll encounter with friends and, if anything, it builds feelings of self-esteem and confidence.

It's normal for siblings to be jealous of and angry at each other from time to time, too. These are generally short-lived emotions. Even when they last longer, they may simply involve a kind of verbal give and take that siblings have adopted as a pattern of relating to each other. Chances are this is more annoying for parents to listen to than detrimental to the relationship between the children.

When there is intense, prolonged, destructive anger between children, it virtually always stems from some parental behavior. If parents neglect their children, siblings may become greedily competitive for the little bit of attention that is available, physically or emotionally. If one sibling is unjustly favored by one or both parents, usually for reasons having nothing to do with the child, that certainly can ignite feelings of envious anger in another child. Sometimes parents don't recognize the uniqueness of each child in the family, maybe even priding themselves on treating all their children with strict equality; but if kids have very different needs, this can stimulate acrimonious rivalry. Parents also may make unfair comparisons between two of their children or even overtly encourage unhealthy competition between kids.

All of these situations make children angry and rightly so. What son who's gifted with athletic talent wants to be told that the intellectual pursuits of his older sister have a higher value in the family? What sister wants to hear over and over that her brother's been chosen yet again to accompany Dad on his Saturday errands? What child wants to feel that she's fallen short if she doesn't get the same grades as her brothers and sisters, or that her straight hair and slightly buck teeth are a problem, unlike her sister's beauty queen looks? No child wants to be told he's defective because he hates the family's yearly camping trips, or that she'll never play the saxophone the way her brother did when she'd prefer to have gymnastics lessons in the first place.

Justifiably angry at their parents for placing them

in situations like these, kids get mad at a sibling instead, which feels less dangerous and threatening. These are the true origins of the phenomenon of sibling rivalry. It doesn't simply come with the territory of being human and having a brother or sister.

# PART THREE

## Need Help?

# CHAPTER EIGHT

# The Anger Metamorphosis and Its Legacies

We all mishandle children's anger sometimes. It's not humanly possible to do otherwise. However, if we're able and willing to recognize our mistakes, we can learn from them and strengthen our bond with our children at the same time. It's not hard to figure out that a child's angry when we're paying attention and observing carefully. The signs are obvious. When we understand that the anger reflects an underlying distress and that we needn't feel threatened by it, we can be there to offer help.

For some parents, however, this seems nearly impossible. They don't simply mishandle their children's angry feelings occasionally, their own difficulties with anger cause them to do it repeatedly.

The parent may be completely unconscious of this pattern. Perhaps she's rationalized away the need to question her behavior. It really doesn't matter to the child, though. Either way, he loses out, and the loss is profound.

Children whose anger is continually mishandled receive the definite message that anger is not a normal, natural emotion, but it is unacceptable. This message sets in motion a complex psychological process I call the *anger metamorphosis*.

## THE ANGER METAMORPHOSIS

The anger metamorphosis is an insidious process that develops over the years. Fortunately, there are many opportunities along the way that can alert us that this process is under way. This is important to remember because the process can be reversed— more easily at its beginning, with more effort later on.

After healthy anger has been repeatedly mishandled by important people in the child's environment, the metamorphosis has started. Again, it is the long-term mishandling that initiates this process and not the occasional mishandling that happens in all households from time to time.

The anger metamorphosis consists of the following stages:

### Stage One

A child may try even harder to get her normal message of need across. In such cases, we would see heightened signs of anger or exaggerated expressions of normal anger. The child is caught in an agonizing and destructive situation when even the heightened anger remains unanswered. This further distress causes her sense of helplessness and frustration to grow and, along with it, her anger. When she expresses this now compounded anger, it's mishandled once again. This vicious circle plays a major part in the anger metamorphosis.

## Stage Two

She begins trying to curtail her open expression of anger. When she feels mad, she attempts to control it. She doesn't display it as she used to. This is usually done increasingly automatically—out of awareness of the child.

This hiding of a normal human emotion has great ramifications, even beyond sparking the anger metamorphosis. As stated previously, whenever any of us buries or tries to do away with a natural part of our emotional system, we suffer something that's like an amputation. The effect on our psyches is just as great as losing a limb would be on our bodies. The difference is that we're not always aware of the deficits that the emotional loss causes. If we had an arm cut off, for instance, we would notice its absence constantly as we struggled to dress ourselves, to cut our food, to perform countless daily tasks. The effects of cutting off anger aren't as obvious, but they're just as real. Thus, this loss of the ability to express anger in a straightforward way effectively deprives children of one of the most important tools they have to convey a need for help. As a result, the child is also robbed of the chance to develop security and trust in caring and supportive figures in the environment and in herself.

## Stage Three

Since direct anger has not gotten the desired response, children will now try other behaviors. Such behaviors as trying extra hard to please, becoming cunningly manipulative, or silently complying with whatever a parent asks are some examples. Any behavior that might get a response is tried. A child might choose to excel in areas in which she knows the mishandling parent is interested, such as academics, sports, computers, or social life. This isn't being done out of a natural desire, but more to garner the parents' attention. As such, these activities take on a driven quality and are out of touch with deeper and truer currents of the child's nature.

In this stage, we begin to see early signs of more serious psychiatric disturbance. These signs are usually transient and quite mild, but they are clear signals of disturbance. Signs might include passing symptoms of nervousness, bad moods, changes in sleep pattern, some bodily complaints, school problems, bedwetting or soiling, unusual eating patterns, passing substance experimentation, allusions to suicide, or other unusual, troubling phenomena. These pass quickly and are the forerunners of the more ingrained, full-blown psychiatric disturbances, which

I call the **legacies of mishandled anger**. These legacies are the result of a more complete metamorphosis.

## Stage Four

The child begins to bury her anger through the mechanism of repression. Although she has tried before to control her anger by conscious will, now this more radical solution is attempted.

Repression is a way of dealing with feelings that we consider dangerous or unacceptable. It consists of banishing them from our awareness, automatically and unconsciously, so that we often don't even know we're doing it. This doesn't mean that the feelings no longer exist. They continue, in fact, to lead an active subterranean life, affecting us in all sorts of ways, even though they're now beyond our awareness.

A child who arrives at the repression stage in the anger metamorphosis believes that he's free of the anger that's been building up and threatening to explode. This seems to decrease the risk of provoking further anger in his parents, an equally great threat. No child wants to feel that he's been exiled from his parents' good graces. Burying his anger, in fact, seems like a way to break the vicious circle that he's trapped in. All it really does, of course, is to remove the child's conscious anger, and the problem remains, not only unsolved, but more deeply rooted than ever. The child's angry feelings will continue to have an effect, but now he won't realize it.

Once embarked on this project of burying anger, children also employ other mental mechanisms to keep anger out. Most commonly, the child externalizes anger as the next step. Externalization is a psychological device that we employ to shift to the outside world what are really inner feelings. When a child externalizes anger, for example, he no longer feels that he's angry, but he often feels that other people are. This seems to confirm to him that he's eliminated his dangerous anger, but it also makes the world seem a more perilous place than it really is.

At this point, a child whose sense of security is already shaky because he's repressing his anger now feels even more threatened by outside forces as well—another vicious circle. This, of course, further erodes his notion of his identity. His uncertainty about who he is deepens; he doesn't know what he can expect from other people. His insecurity and confusion grow by leaps and bounds. He experiences anxiety and fear with greater intensity because he worries more about the anger he feels all around him. He also worries more, because repressing anger is, itself, a cause of anxiety.

## Stage Five

Now he's reached the fifth and final stage of the anger metamorphosis. The original anger—appropriate, natural, communicative—that he has controlled, repressed, and externalized finally becomes expanded anxiety, hostility, and rage.

These end products of the anger metamorphosis bear no resemblance to the original anger. Its aims were constructive, it didn't leave scars, it enhanced the child's relations with others, and it was transient. Buried hostility and rage, on the other hand, are destructive. These feelings become the main fuels of a host of different psychiatric disturbances.

The child, of course, continues even more to call upon repression in order to bury these end products. If his original anger came to seem dangerous to him, think of how hazardous the hostility and rage must feel. If he were to express these even more vitriolic feelings, he'd surely lose anything that remains of his relationships with the adults in his world. In response, he buries these feelings as well, his anxiety enlarges, and the vicious circles he's trapped in continue to expand and strengthen.

Occasionally, children aren't able to keep this painful state of anxiety and hostility buried by employing additional repression. They can't keep the lid clamped on and they act out their aggressive feelings and thoughts. Their rage and hostility is no secret to anyone who crosses their paths.

However, it's much more common for children whose anger is continually mishandled to undergo the anger metamorphosis I've described. Once this process is completed, the buried hostility and rage and the anxiety that comes along with them lie like poisons in a well beneath the surface of everything a child does. The well can produce only toxic effects.

We've all read about toxic waste dumps that eventually leak their poisons into the soil and water around them. The people who live near such sites finally suffer the physical effects of this proximity.

The toxic effects of the poisoned well left by the anger metamorphosis take a different form. Children suffer mental problems that include various symptoms and habits, behavior abnormalities, and personality disorders. Occasionally, the damage to their emotions even causes physical disease. I'll discuss these legacies of mishandled anger in the following section.

## THE LEGACIES OF MISHANDLED ANGER

Over the years, I've treated many young people suffering from afflictions such as school failure, family issues, worries about physical disease, suicide, sleep and eating disorders, troubling moods and behaviors, and disturbing thoughts.

Of course, the anger metamorphosis isn't the sole factor explaining the complex phenomena of a full-blown psychiatric disturbance. Many different forces play a part in a child's developing problems. Biological heritage may be a factor predisposing a youngster to a particular sort of difficulty, and certainly the specific family environment is important.

However, psychiatric difficulties, to a large degree, are the result of mishandled anger, and these legacies are invariably malignant.

When reading about these psychiatric difficulties, keep in mind that I have described the legacies as full-blown, completely formed psychiatric syndromes. In real life, only a small minority of children ever present themselves in such pure fashion. For the great majority of children who have developed a legacy, most of the aspects of the described difficulty exist along with many other normal and abnormal traits.

We don't really know precisely why one child will develop the legacy of depression, for example, while another will have an eating disorder instead. The reason a particular type of problem manifests itself is a complex one and probably has to do with a combination of genetic predisposition, family influences, and cultural norms.

The legacies of mishandled anger generally show themselves in three different ways: psychiatric symptoms, exaggerated personality traits, and behavioral disturbances.

The psychiatric symptoms most closely allied to the anger metamorphosis are:

- Depression
- Sleep disorders
- Bodily disorders
- Speech disorders
- Anxiety disorders
- Suicidal tendencies
- Eating disorders

- Psychosis
- Chronic boredom

Exaggerated personality traits that often arise from mishandled anger include:

- Overdependence
- Overindependence
- Aggression
- Compulsiveness

Among the behavioral disturbances linked with buried anger are:

- Accident proneness
- Bedwetting and soiling
- School failure
- Substance abuse
- Addictions such as consumerism, sex, hobbies, working out, gambling, playing video games
- Competitiveness
- Stealing

For the purposes of this book, I have presented these legacies as rather neat packages. In reality, children don't come with all the loose ends tied up, so keep in mind that the legacies of the anger metamorphosis may not fit into tidy categories. Sometimes they overlap, with a child showing more than one at a time; sometimes a child may exhibit one legacy during the school age period, and an entirely different one as an adolescent.

Most important to remember is that legacy formation is a constant process and thus can be affected by your constructive handling of anger at any time.

## Psychiatric Symptoms

*Depression.* Although professionals in the mental health fields have been slow to accept the fact, depression does happen in kids, and it happens frequently.

Depression is indicated by one or more of the following markers: sadness, hopelessness, despair, physical lethargy, thoughts of suicide, guilt, low self-esteem, decreased appetite, insomnia or hypersomnia, difficulty concentrating, and social or scholastic difficulties including withdrawal into isolation and outright failure.

*Stuart, was eight when his parents brought him to see me. He'd told them he wanted to jump out of his fifth story window, and then "be run over, squashed, and taken away to the garbage dump." Given such feelings, it wasn't surprising that I saw in him many of the classic signs of depression. This behavior began not long after Stuart's much-loved maternal grandfather died. Stuart really wanted to be reunited with his grandfather, whom he missed terribly and at whom he was also angry. His parents didn't con-*

*nect his anger with his grandfather's death and
his feelings of abandonment. Quite quickly, Stuart began to mishandle his own anger. His buried
hostility showed up in depression.*

**Sleep disorders.** Sleep is one of the best indicators we have of our mental state. When we're at
peace, we sleep pretty well. When we have problems,
sleep is one of the first areas to be disturbed. This is
true for children as well as adults. Buried anger can
play havoc with a good night's sleep.

Sleep disturbances cover a lot of territory, all the
way from fear of the dark to sleepwalking and night
terrors. In between these extremes are trouble going
to sleep, bedtime rituals, nightmares, and sleeping
too little (insomnia) or too much (hypersomnia). Although current research indicates that there may be
some physiological basis for certain sleep problems,
it's been my experience that a child who's having
sleep difficulties is nearly always the victim of mishandled anger.

Night terrors may have a physiological compo-
nent. Even so, I don't think we should ignore the
panic, anguish, and even occasional violence that occur during these nighttime events as indicators of
mishandled anger as well.

**Bodily disorders.** That buried anger can wreak
havoc on children's bodies shouldn't come as a great
surprise. For years, we've known that emotional upsets can affect physical health, and there's been a lot

of research done and anecdotal evidence gathered about this. It is now accepted that emotional difficulties are often expressed through bodily organs and that the predisposition toward this type of expression often has a genetic root.

The following physical complaints and problems are quite common and often associated with buried anger: headaches, muscle cramps and spasms, teeth-grinding, dermatitis (particularly eczema), ulcers, colitis, diarrhea, abdominal pain, heartburn, nausea, asthma, hyperventilation, fainting, obesity, chronic colds, chronic fatigue, menstrual irregularities, dizziness, ringing in the ears, loss of hearing and/or sight, tics, early feeding difficulties, and some cases of colic. Keep in mind, however, that every instance of diarrhea isn't a sign of anger that's been buried, nor is underground hostility the only cause of nausea or menstrual irregularities. Some physical problems may even have multiple causes.

*Speech disorders.* The way we speak may often reveal more about our emotions than the words we use. It's not hard to spot depression in someone whose speech is slow and sparse, for instance. Anxious speech, on the other hand, has a rapid, driven quality, as though it were being propelled by a high-pressure engine. Tense people whose aggression is barely under wraps may have a staccato speech pattern. Kids who stutter and stammer, have a hard time articulating words, or suffer from other childhood speech disorders often have a problem with buried anger.

*Anxiety disorders.* There's no disputing the intimate link between anger and anxiety. These words even share similar roots in some ancient languages.

Some children experience this terribly painful feeling quite directly. They're the worriers, fretting over absolutely everything. They're tense, sometimes hypochondriacal, and even given to full-fledged panic attacks when they're forced into certain situations. This sort of general and constant nervousness can truly cripple a child as it pushes her constantly toward the fringes of life.

Other children may exhibit anxiety in more limited and distinct ways. One child may be anxious about social interactions, for example, or about separations from home and familiar people. In more complicated cases, a child may suffer from the irrational fears we call phobias, such as the fear of everyday situations or objects such as animals, heights, or crowds. Another child might worry herself sick with anxiety-provoking intrusive thoughts, questions, or pathologically doubting almost anything. These characteristics are known as obsessions. Still another youngster might be the victim of habitual compulsive behavior such as the need to wash constantly, to check doors and windows, to touch certain things, or to perform certain rituals.

*Suicide.* This most serious of all the mental health problems that children face becomes particularly prominent in midadolescence and peaks when young people are in their early twenties. According to statistics, it's a problem that seems to be growing. I'm sure that if the accidental deaths of adolescents were included in these statistics—as they often should be—the rates of teenage suicide would be even higher.

Although young adults have the highest risk of suicide, it does happen at younger ages as well. Certainly any child who reports suicidal feelings or makes any kind of suicide attempt should receive immediate professional attention. In fact, my feeling is that a professional should see any child who seems preoccupied or overly concerned with thoughts of death, who doesn't function well because of those thoughts, or who has other psychiatric symptoms that go along with the thoughts, such as a feeling of hopelessness.

A child who feels hopeless is convinced that, no matter what she does, no matter how she tries to communicate her distress, she'll be met by the same ineffective, unhelpful response she's always received. Her parents or other adults in her world won't recognize what's really going on. They never have, so why should they now? In other words, she believes they'll mishandle her anger once again. That anger, which has been buried and building for some time, is now extremely powerful.

When such a child suffers what she considers a

failure or setback of some kind, however trivial it may seem to the outsider, the stage is set for suicide. The youngster may not have a well-developed idea of death and may not understand how absolutely final it is. That doesn't matter. What death seems to offer is an inviting end to pain. Suicide may also appear to a child as a fitting act of revenge against an uncaring world, one that never acknowledged her pain in the first place and never offered any way out of it.

No suicide attempt should ever be taken lightly, although I've seen both professionals and parents do just this. Perhaps they dismiss the attempt as an impulsive aberration, or a mere act of retaliation.

Glimpsing the suicidal potential in a youngster frightens us, just as anger often does. Like anger, it activates our psychological defenses. If we notice in our children any of the signs I've listed above, we must pay attention. No matter how frightening a suicide attempt is for us as parents, it's too often fatal for our kids.

Despite our fairly advanced knowledge about children's mental health, it's still impossible to predict a suicidal act or to explain satisfactorily why one child and not another might try suicide. There are certain signs and/or events that can alert us to the increased risk of suicide in our kids. These are:

- An unusual change in behavior, mood, or thinking, such as withdrawal from friends and activities
- A sudden decline in school performance
- An increase in dangerous behaviors, such as dare-

devil stunts, speeding in a car, or fighting
- Depression
- Bizarre behavior that's a sign of severe mental illness, such as hallucinations or strange thoughts
- Talk about death or suicide, or written evidence that they're on a child's mind (a suicide note, for instance, or a diary including poems about death, such as the mother of a suicidal patient of mine found open on her child's desk)

Seek help for your child immediately, especially if these indicators are present in combination with a recent social setback; an illness; painful circumstances such as parental absence, geographic upheaval, or child abuse; a prior psychiatric history (particularly if it has included past brushes with suicide); recent separations from important people through death or illness; and substance abuse.

*Eating disorders.* The most common of these abnormal eating patterns are anorexia nervosa and bulimia nervosa, and they afflict teenagers more than any other age group. It's not unusual to see both of these syndromes in the same child. It's also common, beneath the dramatic surface of both disorders, to find other problems that revolve around buried anger.

It may seem obvious that an eating problem reflects greater underlying difficulties, but frequently it isn't obvious to patients I've seen or to their parents. Our culture, after all, encourages a fierce concentration on bodily size and being thin is its maxim.

But the problems that underlie eating disorders are evident not only in a teenager's obsession with weight, eating, and body image, but in something that goes with the obsession: the inability to experience pleasure. That has convinced me, as much as anything else, of the presence of buried anger beneath these legacies. The anger metamorphosis, which results from efforts to cut off the experience of anger, necessarily disposes of other feelings as well, particularly fun and pleasure. And in my experience, nowhere is this more evident than in patients with eating disorders.

*Psychosis.*  The most profound of all mental disorders, psychosis can appear in youngsters, though it happens more often in adults. Very young children suffer from psychoses known as pervasive developmental disorders, which includes autistism as well as other varieties. Schizophrenia and manic depression are more likely to appear during adolescence and involve a child losing touch with reality and often experiencing hallucinations (false perceptions— seeing, hearing, feeling, tasting, or smelling things that aren't there) and delusions (false and sometimes bizarre beliefs) as well. Obviously, with disturbances like these, kids can't function, think, or behave in the usual ways. In fact, they often look and act quite abnormally, even freakish, which is hardly surprising.

*Chronic boredom.* A lack of interest in or excitement about anything, internal or external, and zero motivation to get involved in any kind of activity mean to me that a child has become disconnected from her vital inner self. The anger metamorphosis always threatens a child's sense of well-being, and it automatically involves diminishing emotional awareness.

Kids who suffer from chronic boredom have lost all sense of aliveness. Not only has the anger metamorphosis dimmed their sense of anger, it has taken the edge off experiencing life in general. All of their reactions are blunted. Boredom seems like the sole end product of a life filled with anger.

Often, when I visit the adolescent inpatient psychiatric wards, I meet teenagers who complain constantly about how bored they are. These same kids won't do anything that might relieve their boredom. This paralysis acts as a protection against intensely painful feelings that lurk just below the surface, especially feelings of impotent rage.

## Exaggerated Personality Traits

Our personalities are made up of traits, or qualities, that reflect the way we think, feel, behave, perceive the world, and interact with it. Ideally, we're able to use all of these traits flexibly, rather than being rigidly wedded to one or a few. In adulthood, people who lack this flexibility, who are governed mainly by one characteristic to the apparent exclusion of others, are diagnosed with personality disorders labeled narcissistic, paranoid, antisocial, and so on. This simply means that one aspect of their personality so dominates the others that they appear to be run by only that quality.

It's harder to diagnose personality disorders in children, because they're still growing and changing. Their patterns, we hope, haven't yet calcified the way they have in some adults. Unfortunately, it's not uncommon to find youngsters who exhibit something that looks very similar to this adult phenomenon. One aspect of these children's personalities overshadows all the others.

Children with exaggerated personality traits don't, in any full and free sense, choose one quality to govern them, of course. They are driven to this modus operandi by the anxiety, buried hostility, and rage that result from the anger metamorphosis. A single aspect of their personality comes to dominate the others in response to the mishandling of their anger. Their chosen trait provides them with the illusion that their anger is under control, and their anxiety level is down.

***The dependent child.*** The dependent child feels frightened, anxious, and generally helpless in most situations. She often turns for help to someone she sees as more powerful, because at some time she sensed that emphasizing her neediness and incompetence would mute her anger, make it less threatening and, therefore, make it less likely to be "offensive" and mishandled.

It's common for kids who appear fearful and blundering to be picked on by other children. Dependent children, who feel and act weak and ineffectual, actually invite treatment from others that makes them feel even more inadequate.

Generally, the methods of mishandling anger most likely to produce a dependent child are those that strictly forbid the expression of angry feelings or those that try to safeguard a child against them through overprotection.

*The aggressive child.* The anger this child feels is no surprise to anyone because he acts it out at the drop of a hat. It's as though his buried anger, now converted to hostility and rage, refused to stay in the grave, blasted the lid off the coffin, and fought through the earth to get to the surface. Once it arrives there and the child begins spreading it around with seeming relish, his acting out may be called a variety of things: oppositional, conduct problem, and behavior disorder are among the labels.

Aggressive children usually come from homes that have been disrupted—perhaps one parent is absent—that have a harsh, punitive atmosphere, or that have a parent who's secretly gratified by the child's behavior. The aggression may show up in many different ways.

The oppositional child, for example, might use

passive-aggressive ploys (I won't do it because you say so), defiance and disobedience, frequent arguments or, if pushed to the wall, temper tantrums. The child who shows aggression more directly might bully or tease others, humiliate them, be cruel, vindictive, or violent. Antisocial acts such as fire setting, lying, and cheating are still other forms of aggression. Aggressive kids may seem to take pleasure in labeling themselves "toughs," trodding on the rights of others with a seemingly untroubled conscience. Their acts can be callous and uncaring.

Less obvious, but sometimes just as aggressive, is the child who's a compulsive achiever, who lords her accomplishments over others, who shows off continually, and is a fierce competitor.

Whatever form the aggression takes, these children seem unable to be anything but angry. Usually, their angry feelings have been mishandled with more harshness than exists in some of the other legacies. They try just as hard as other kids to bury their anger during the anger metamorphosis, but, almost invariably, their anger is being intensely and continually stimulated at the same time. Ultimately, it's too powerful for them to push down beneath the surface and it detonates with considerable force.

Contrary to appearances, these youngsters do have consciences. They feel guilty about their behavior. Sometimes, in fact, their consciences are so strict that they rebel against them, along with everything else. Their rebellious, disruptive behavior frequently prevents them from being in regular schools, which aren't equipped to handle the problems these kids present. It's not unusual to find them in special institutions or even in jail when they're quite young.

Another, and common, sort of aggressive child is the put-down artist. This child becomes a master of the insult, with a highly developed perception about the weaknesses of others. Those vulnerable areas are where she strikes, often with razor sharp, sarcastic wisecracks, frequently playing to the crowd in an exhibitionistic way. She's also a specialist in gossip, humiliation, and jokes, always at the expense of another child.

In fact, though it may not seem so, her real aim and interest is lifting herself up in order to combat the inferiority she feels due to her mishandled anger. When confronted with the effects of her behavior on others, she may be genuinely surprised.

*The independent child.* Independence is valued in our culture and parents hope to instill this capacity in their children. We want our kids to be able to think and act for themselves, not to be swayed by the crowd, to live up to their unique inner potential, and to be able to experience solitude and its rewards. However, the independence born of buried anger doesn't accomplish any of these things.

Just as the dependent child adopts a posture of needy incompetence as a barrier against further anger and its mishandling, so the independent child settles on keeping his distance from others as the safest course. He feels this safety zone will buffer him from added distress.

Independence becomes a problem when it leads to social and emotional isolation, frequently stimulates excessive daydreaming and fantasizing, and promotes shyness, reclusiveness, and the coldness that comes from shutting down nearly all feelings. The independent child can't form meaningful attachments and generally drifts toward the fringes of human activity.

Ultimately, this child doesn't really seem to express much of anything, especially anger. She may seem out of it, a "space cadet," as the expression goes. The anger is still there, however deeply buried. Should it show itself—usually in an uncharacteristic burst of aggression—it seems particularly strange coming from this child because we don't expect it. We've become used to her bland, disconnected surface.

*The compulsive child.* What happens when a child's entire personality is dominated by the quality of compulsiveness? Generally, he is a perfectionist who has very high behavior standards, both for himself and others. Since these standards are virtually impossible to meet, and everyone falls short, he's often angry at himself and those around him.

This child's anger seldom mars his good behavior. He follows rules and regulations, almost to a fault, and also pays meticulous attention to details and to cleanliness. This isn't a kid who's having much fun in life, and his peers know it. They're likely to see him as a drag, a wet blanket, a joyless watchdog, and they'd rather not have him around. He starts to feel excluded and grows angrier still.

Their goal of perfection and their intense focus on details often undermine the very thing compulsive children are trying to achieve. In school, for example, they may be torn by indecisiveness. What should they study first? How should they study it? What's the best approach? How can the project be completed perfectly? As with the other exaggerated personality traits, once compulsivity is in the driver's seat, other aspects of the child's personality wither away from disuse.

## Behavior disturbances

Children with behavior disturbances are sometimes referred to as "acting out" types, which simply means that they experience and express their emotional problems primarily in the sphere of behavioral activity. They can be particularly challenging for anyone trying to understand them—their parents, outsiders, and themselves—because everyone focuses almost exclusively on their behavior. As time goes on, the underlying issues, especially anger mishandling, become more and more obscured and harder to get at.

*Accident proneness.* For a long time, accident proneness was thought to grow out of a self-destructive drive. While that's sometimes true, accidents also can be part of a far more complicated process than that catch phrase indicates.

In a minority of cases, a child feels guilty about his buried anger and precipitating an accident serves, unconsciously, as punishment. It may also sometimes satisfy a need for revenge toward those who didn't respond helpfully to his original anger.

It's far more common for kids to have frequent accidents because they're preoccupied and distracted by the anxiety they feel. This anxiety, a by-product of the anger metamorphosis, keeps them from paying attention. They're engrossed in the struggle to bury their anger, even as they're aware that it keeps accumulating, no matter what they do. This preoccupation causes them to ignore certain safety mechanisms that most children would use automatically.

*Bedwetting and soiling.* These are complex problems and many opinions exist about what causes them and how they should be treated. Young children may express natural, appropriate, transient anger through slip-ups in these areas, but long-term bedwetting and soiling may also be expressions of buried anger, indicating a more serious problem.

Whatever the cause, bedwetting and soiling cause great shame and anger in children. If these incidents continue for any period of time, the children grow extremely angry with themselves for their loss of control. This anger is piled on top of the buried angry feelings that may have caused the bedwetting or soiling in the first place.

If a child can't get through a night without wetting or soiling his bed, it starts to limit the things he can do. Sleeping over at a friend's house becomes risky; going to camp is dangerous. These limitations undermine the child's self-confidence and self-esteem further, and add to his anger and humiliation. Any child who displays this behavior over time should receive a psychiatric consultation in order to explore whether or not buried anger is part of the problem.

*School failure.* School is where most children spend the bulk of their time when they're not home. Not only do nearly all of the legacies make an appearance during school at some point, anger problems can also interfere with a child's ability to learn and perform scholastically.

When a child isn't doing well in school, the first step should be a thorough evaluation of all aspects of the learning process: physical, psychological, and educational. If the psychological red flag goes up, buried anger should always be considered as a possible cause of difficulty. The following are just some of the ways that school failure may be a legacy of mishandled anger.

- A child's defiant, oppositional behavior against his parents continues at school. School demands compliance with authority, after all, and the child may balk at this.

- A child's rebellion may be less overt. Perhaps she behaves passive-aggressively, by not doing assignments on time, forgetting her books, or arriving late at class.

- To the dependent child who's buried his anger beneath a veneer of infantilism and helplessness, learning may represent an assertion of independence that's beyond him. He can't risk it.

- An overly competitive child who's been called on the carpet for behaving too competitively as a reaction to buried hostility may now fear how the other kids will view her. She may recoil from learning to show that she's really not a threat at all.

- Related to the above may be the fear-of-success syndrome we've all heard of. This can occur when learning has been equated with an act of aggression against a sibling, for example, or even against a parent. Unconsciously fearing retaliation, this child may fail in school.

*Substance abuse.*  Young people often begin to use drugs and alcohol in order to relieve the psychic pain they feel. Most addicted youngsters, in fact, recall that the first time they had a drink, smoked marijuana, or used some other drug, they immediately felt better. Their mishandled anger, conflicts, bad mood, shyness, or feeling of being different from others seemed to recede; they felt equipped to cope with their feelings and closer to being the person they wished they were; or they simply didn't care as much about what went on around them. Their suffering was numbed, even if only temporarily. What begins as an effort at pain relief may last a lifetime during which none of the underlying problems get solved.

*Other addictions.* Drugs and alcohol aren't the only things that young people who've buried their anger become addicted to. While some of the following activities aren't as potent or lethal as ingesting mind-altering substances, they serve some of the same purposes. They may be welcome distractions from a child's difficulties, a way to blot out feelings, change a child's mood, or they may become avenues for releasing some of the buried hostility that comes to feel unbearable.

Consumerism is an intense focus on buying material goods, especially clothing, and I think this trend is growing as advertising and telecommunications make deep inroads into our young population. Current fads and a family's finances determine what children consume, and today the most popular items, apart from clothing, seem to be video games, electronic devices, tapes, and compact discs.

All children today are exposed to the consumer-oriented climate that exists throughout our culture, but I've found that the children doing the most compulsively driven sort of buying are those who carry around buried anger. The latest video, the hottest sneakers, the newest boom box—whatever kids choose—seem temporarily to soothe the distress and anger that these children feel.

• • •

The legacy of sex addiction usually appears when a child has been sexually stimulated early in life by seductive behavior from an adult, overt sexual abuse, or by exposure to sexual material in some form. It may show itself in promiscuity, Don Juanism (the compulsion to seduce and conquer) or precocious sexuality.

Sex addiction has little to do with erotic pleasure. It's much more often a way of rebelling against authority or a desperate grab for human contact by a child who's feeling increasingly helpless and isolated as the prospects of help dwindle.

The sexual expression of buried anger only increases young people's problems, of course, just as all of the legacies do. It earns kids a poor reputation, their relationships with people deteriorate, they become more isolated, and their focus becomes narrower. Also, sex addiction increases the risks that the youngster will become pregnant, contract a sexually transmitted disease, or be subjected to violence and/or abuse by partners.

Our society, as I've noted, puts great stock in appearances. Due to that, I think, compulsive working out is starting earlier and earlier in children's lives. Although this usually turns up in boys, it's not their exclusive territory.

Angry young teenagers generally begin lifting weights to overcome a sense of distress about feelings of inferiority. These kids focus on their bodies, perhaps because of the cultural emphasis on appearances and the message that if you look good, everything else will fall into place.

Quite quickly, though, these youngsters can become consumed by the pursuit of burgeoning muscles, devoting every spare moment to going to the gym or exercising on home equipment, and they let all other activities lapse. It's as though they come to equate their worth with their muscle size. An obsessive focus on certain aerobic activities is also a common sign of buried anger.

Video games are fashionable for children in our society, and a great deal has been written about their effects, both good and bad, on children's development. Video game addiction can also be a legacy of mishandled anger.

Children can spend entire days in front of the television set or in arcades playing these games. Like any other addiction, this temporarily dulls angry feelings, and the violent, destructive themes of some of the games makes them expressions of inner angry feelings. I haven't seen many video games dwelling on cooperation, growth, and love that have gone straight to the top of the charts.

A child's hobby can serve as a great prod to development. Hobbies can be enriching and rewarding. How do you tell the difference between a harmless hobby and hobby addiction?

An addiction exists when a hobby seems to have

the child rather than the other way around. Does your daughter come in from school, go directly to the computer, and stay there for the rest of the day and night, allowing herself to be dragged away only for dinner and, eventually, bedtime? Does your son spend every spare moment with his stamp collection, poring over stamp magazines, writing away for stamps, going through stamp albums, prowling through shops that carry stamps? Do both of them refuse to take breaks for phone calls from friends, family activities, to go to the movies, to do anything else? It's the driven and exclusive nature of a child's pursuit of a hobby that can alert a parent to its addictive nature.

Earlier I mentioned that competitiveness can be a sign of anger that occurs in the normal course of a child's development. Compulsive competition can be distinguished from the normal, healthy variety when it seems indiscriminate—a child appears driven to compete in virtually any area, not just those where she has special skills, talents, or interests. When losing causes an extremely angry reaction in the child, it can also be identified as compulsive. Finally, competitiveness is compulsive when it prevents a child from doing something because she's afraid she might lose.

Often, stealing is a passing phase in children who are angry at one thing or another. Even though it does pass, however, like any sign of anger, it indicates an underlying distress that needs attention. When stealing becomes chronic, it can definitely be considered a legacy of mishandled anger.

Most often, chronic, compulsive stealing is based on long-standing feelings of rage induced in a child by neglect. Other angry behavior, usually of an aggressive nature, can also go along with stealing. When that's true, the stealing is most likely just a part of a child's more widespread antisocial attitudes.

Sometimes stealing stands alone as a legacy. Then it's helpful to explore the timing of the stealing, who's being stolen from, and what's being stolen. These can offer clues that often reveal the source of the buried anger.

## HOW TO TELL IF A LEGACY HAS TAKEN HOLD

The legacies of mishandled anger are all serious and all deserve special attention, but many kids show fleeting glimpses of legacylike behavior without really having serious problems. How can parents tell when they have a real crisis on their hands? If a child's disturbance meets several of the following criteria, it is probable that a legacy has been established.

- Duration: The problem's been going on for some time, usually months.
- Intensity: It has a vehemence, power, and tenacity.

- Amenability to correction: No attempted superficial solution has worked.
- The problem is not understandable: The parent can't link the child's behavior to a specific anger-inducing situation. In other words, the legacy has taken hold based on anger being buried and metamorphosized.

Children pay dearly for any of the malignant legacies of mishandled anger. What at one point seems to them like a solution—burying their angry feelings—turns out to be quite the opposite. Their problems increase; their helplessness and hostility grow; their "solution" may even destroy them. At the very least, they become so locked in by the compulsive nature of the legacy that they're robbed of their ability to make choices. They forfeit their emotional freedom and, along with it, the capacity for vital change and spontaneity. When that happens, they've lost any chance of developing a genuine self.

Keep in mind the following facts about anger metamorphosis and the formation of legacies.

- Legacy formation is a gradual process that happens after repetitive mishandling of anger.
- Many children exhibit fleeting symptoms of legacies but only when the symptom has the duration, intensity, unamenability to change and seems to be disconnected from what you understand should you conclude that a legacy exists.

- In the early stages of the anger metamorphosis, the intervention of constructive handling of anger can reverse the process.
- In the later stages and after the establishment of a legacy, reversal is still possible with a better understanding of the child's anger and the reasons for its mismanagement. This often necessitates professional help.

# CHAPTER NINE

# Seeking Professional Help

By the time people decide to seek professional help, a child's problems are likely to be pretty well entrenched. A long period of mishandled anger usually precedes their phone call; the anger metamorphosis is under way; frequently, mishandled angry feelings have already been buried and converted; legacies may have appeared. More often than not, people have tried every way they know to solve the problem before appearing in my office. As much as I might wish it were otherwise—a problem caught early is more easily solved, and the pain and damage involved is decidedly less—I'm afraid this is simply human nature.

It's like treating a physical complaint with home remedies before conceding that the ailment isn't responding, is perhaps getting worse, and that expert help may be called for. The child psychiatrist is frequently the last resort, the person people seek out when all else has failed. We all like to think we can handle things on our own, especially when it comes to parenting.

Despite the fact that most of us approach the major challenge of being a parent with no on-the-job training, we tend to consider ourselves experts. Who knows our children better than we do, after all? Also, because we have the notion that the difficult job of raising a child is supposed to come naturally, we may think that seeking help is a weakness or shortcoming. Finally, as with other circumstances in life, many of us wait until we feel our backs are against the wall before taking what we think of as drastic measures.

Generally, when parents get in touch with me, they describe a specific problem. A teacher has told them that their son is behaving terribly and doing poorly in school; other parents have told them that their daughter is obnoxious and creating trouble when she gets together with her friends; the parents themselves have noticed troubling behavior in their child: their teenager is excessively moody; their seven-year-old panics each morning before leaving for school; a child's occasional nightmares have become more frequent and lurid; what began as a youngster's diet plan to lose a few pounds has become the refusal to eat anything but lettuce and liquids. Perhaps what seemed to be just part of their child's personality has now taken on pathological proportions: their son was always shy, but now he has no social contacts whatsoever; their worrier, who's always been concerned with details and planning, seems suddenly terrified to touch anything in the house; a child known as a troublemaker at school is now involved with the police because of vandalism and drug use.

As well as describing to me the often dramatic issue that prompted the call, parents generally talk about the struggles they've had with the child in their efforts to cure the problem. They've tried quarantining the drug user, but he persists in defying them; they've arranged social activities for their isolated shrinking violet only to be met by an abusive response; they've prepared special meals at home and taken their dieting offspring to interesting restaurants, but she won't touch her food. They've tried to talk to their kids, to cajole them, to punish them. They haven't gotten anywhere.

In other words, in their opening contact with me, parents usually describe the legacies of mishandled anger or legacylike behaviors and the feeling that they've come to the end of their rope with a child's behavior. As we know by now, this is often simply the tip of the iceberg. What they describe is the result of a complex web of personal interactions with their children that has been strongly influenced by the parents' own histories, by anger-inducing behavior toward their kids, by subsequent mishandling of that anger, and by the vicious circle of the anger metamorphosis that eventually turns a child's natural angry feelings into buried hostility and anxiety.

When a helping professional begins to ask questions probing these underlying psychological issues, no matter how delicately, parents often bristle. They become defensive. What I'm asking is inconsequential, they may say; it has nothing to do with the problem. Let's remember why they called in the first place, they may remind me; it wasn't so that they could be analyzed themselves. They're here because Johnny's flunking out of school, or Susie's continuing to wet her bed, or they found a suicide note in Kathy's desk.

But it's precisely the underlying issues—the family history and how the members of a household deal with each other—that hold the key to help. Focusing strictly on the legacy, the immediate problem, the manifestation of the buried anger, can yield very little. If our car develops a rattle, we don't simply muffle the sound. We look under the hood or elsewhere, trace the noise to its cause, and fix the problem at its source. But as parents we often resist taking a similar step when it comes to our children's problems.

To turn away from the surface and look more deeply causes pain, and none of us welcomes that. When parents are dealing with anger in their children, there are a number of things they have to face. First are the painful feelings that many of us have surrounding anger itself, feelings as old as our own childhoods and our relationships with our own parents. Next we must examine the ways in which we might be provoking anger in our children, our imperfections as parents. Finally, there is our own anger. No wonder we put off the moment of reckoning.

It takes courage to face any one of these matters, let alone all of them.

I want to make clear, though, that professional assistance isn't necessary for every anger problem. Some parents will find that self-help is enough for them to handle these problems in a constructive way. Just keep in mind those things that will prevent you from mishandling your child's anger.

- View your child's anger as a normal feeling that indicates a certain amount of distress.
- Respond to this anger without prejudice.
- Explore the meaning and cause of the distress that is inducing the anger.
- Offer appropriate help as discussed in Chapter Six.

How does a parent know when outside help is necessary? Though many of us are inclined to wait until a problem feels desperate, that's not always the best course to follow. Sometimes, for instance, despite all of our efforts and a great deal of awareness, we may remain baffled about the causes of our child's anger. Perhaps because we're deeply involved or have blind spots about ourselves or our children, we're missing something that a third party—someone who's professionally trained, a friend, or even a family member—could spot easily. Why not take advantage of outside help before being driven to the brink?

Another time when it's helpful, though not crucial, for parents to seek professional counseling is when they know they've had trouble handling anger in their own lives. By examining our own history with anger, we may learn what danger signals to watch for in ourselves or how a particular child might re-open old wounds. In a sense, this sort of help is like practicing preventive medicine; it's a kind of consciousness raising about anger.

There are times when professional help for anger problems is mandatory. The crippling legacies of mishandled anger take a long time to develop, and there are always signs along the way. Maybe a child becomes sad more frequently than usual, has more nightmares, seems overly concerned with physical complaints, or behaves with uncharacteristic aggression. These are signs to pay attention to, and getting help for them may prevent a legacy from forming. When we notice these forerunners of legacies, and can't get at or understand the underlying stress, help is needed.

Unquestionably, professional help is mandatory to deal with the intractable legacies described in Chapter Eight. When a legacy exists, it means that a child's anger has been mishandled for a long time and that efforts to cope with it haven't been effective. They may, in fact, have made things worse. It takes a longer time, working at a deeper level, to reverse the destructive behavior that exists in families in these situations, but it can be done.

Professional help is also mandatory when parents see in themselves any of the danger signals outlined in Chapter Three, tip-offs to the rising risk of child abuse. When parents reach this point with their anger, child rearing is likely to deteriorate and the possibility of physical violence is very real. Such situations rarely turn around on their own. With treatment, it's possible to make changes and avoid permanent damage to the child.

Parents who feel that anger at their children is out of control have nothing to be ashamed of and are just as human as the rest of us. There are reasons why they feel this way. Exploring those reasons, coming to understand them, and learning how to cope with negative anger attitudes can lead to lasting change. With help, these parents can become capable of loving and caring for their children in a healthy way.

If you're already involved in an abusive situation with your child, of course intervention is imperative and it should be immediate. The sooner you act, the more likely you are to avoid a true tragedy.


## CHOOSING A PROFESSIONAL

If you've decided to seek help for anger problems, what should you look for in a professional? It's an important choice, deserving of time and patience on a parent's part, and I'd recommend keeping three criteria in mind:

- Professional credentials
- References
- Personal feelings

## Professional Credentials

The mental health professionals most helpful for children and parents who are mired in anger problems are those who have special training in child and adolescent psychiatric disturbances. The training may vary but it ought to include postgraduate studies that have led to accreditation. The types of certification indicating this include, for trained psychiatrists, an additional residency in child and adolescent psychiatry; a doctorate or master's degree in clinical child psychology; a master's degree in social work with special training in childhood and adolescence; and a psychiatric nursing degree with master's level training in child and adolescent psychiatry.

Many professionals with these certifications will also have taken further training in psychoanalysis, which is especially valuable. I've noted throughout the book that many aspects of mishandling anger—attitudes, responses, the anger metamorphosis—lie outside of our awareness. A professional who's trained in psychoanalysis has heightened sensitivity to the underlying, or unconscious, causes of feelings, thoughts, and behavior. This can be enormously helpful in investigating and coming to understand the genesis and history of anger problems.

Generally, when looking for help for your child, I'd advise steering clear of professionals who've been trained to deal only with adult problems.

Among the professionals I've mentioned—all of whom have knowledge of the diagnosis and treatment of children—are there any real differences? Of course.

For example, the child and teenage psychiatrist is the most broadly trained of the four. He's probably best equipped to make a diagnosis of your child's problem, to assess the physical aspects, if any, and to lay out a comprehensive plan for treatment that covers all bases. He's also able to prescribe medication if necessary.

The child psychologist, on the other hand, has extensive training in psychological testing. This puts him in a position to make the most astute evaluation of factors that aren't necessarily apparent in an interview with another sort of therapist, such as the specific intelligence of a child or specific areas of academic/educational weakness.

Social work training focuses on cultural issues and systems theory, as well as general psychology, so you might expect a social worker to have a keen familiarity with the impact of the culture and the family structure on a child.

In some respects, the training of a psychiatric nurse is similar to that of a psychiatrist, although it's not as extensive. She'll have a strong medical background, a broad knowledge of physical conditions that may bear on the problem, and an expertise in the art of diagnosis.

The differences between these professionals will show up primarily in the initial stages of your contact with them. After diagnosis and treatment planning, when it comes to doing actual therapy with children and their families, there's little to distinguish one of these professionals from another. Each is capable of offering equally sound, effective treatment.

Perhaps the only exception might be in cases when the legacy of mishandled anger involves physical disease or requires medication and/or hospitalization. The child or adolescent psychiatrist would be best equipped to handle those cases.

## References

The second factor to consider in choosing a therapist is references. Many different people are in a position to give you these: your pediatrician, a teacher, and a guidance counselor at your child's school, among others. You'll probably learn more about a practitioner's actual style of working either from a therapist's former patients or from the therapist's personal acquaintances. This information can be extremely valuable since you may garner from it an idea of the treatment you and your child would respond to best and find most helpful. You don't get a sense of how a therapist actually dispenses treatment simply by being given a name.

## Personal Feelings

Perhaps nothing is more important in making this choice than your own instincts and feelings. All the credentials in the world don't mean anything if you don't like the therapist, don't respond positively to her, or don't feel that she's reliable. It's a big step to open up your inner life to someone, and it's important that you feel good about the person to whom you give that trust.

If you're new to therapy, keep in mind that it's not unusual at first to be somewhat wary or anxious, but if your uneasiness persists—if you continue to feel uncomfortable with the therapist's personality, the arrangements about scheduling and fees, or anything else, raise the issue for discussion. See how you feel about the way the therapist handles it. You can learn a great deal from interactions like this. If your doubts aren't allayed, remember that you're free to make a change.

Maybe your brother has told you that "this guy is the best in town." Maybe your best friend raves about a particular therapist who turned his daughter's life around. None of that is necessarily important. A therapist who's enormously helpful for one person may be completely ineffective for someone else. Your gut reaction counts, so pay attention to it.

Other factors may also influence how you feel about a therapist. How does she view anger? How has she learned about children? How much time has she really spent with them and under what circumstances? How much of her practice is spent treating kids? Don't be afraid to ask questions like these. Finally, you'll want to pay attention to how human your exchange with the therapist is and how respectful she seems of both your suffering and your capacity to change.

Putting together the information you've drawn from these three sources—credentials, references, and personal feelings—you'll probably make the choice that's right for you. Remember that there's never just one correct choice. There are a great many well-trained therapists available. All of them are different, and most of them are helpful.

A psychiatric evaluation is common at the outset of therapy dealing with children and adolescents. It is during this process that you may feel the therapist is asking irrelevant questions. The evaluation consists of the professional gathering a detailed history of the current problem, of the youngster's development, of the parents, their marriage, their jobs, the atmosphere in the home and family, and any other aspect of life that may yield clues about what's causing the problem. An inquiry into the strengths of each family member and an account of those areas in which things are going well is equally important.

When a child is very young, most of this history obviously comes from the parents. Older youngsters and teenagers can usually tell their own stories. With teenagers, in fact, the therapist may not even want to see the parents for some time, particularly if the issues of trust and independence are contentious ones between parent and child. In these instances, it's important for the therapist to establish a good working relationship with the adolescent before the parents are even brought into the therapeutic situation.

With young children, once the parents have given a history, the therapist will see the child. If the child is preverbal or is otherwise uncomfortable simply talking, there are other ways for the professional to communicate with the child, such as playing together, reading, writing, drawing, and sharing music. What the professional looks for—whatever the child's age—is both the youngster's strengths and his psychiatric problems. Occasionally, the evaluation may include a family interview in order for the therapist to see the interactions that occur when everyone's together.

The history gathering that comes from interviews—sometimes several separate ones—and the examination of the child, as well as any necessary physical or psychological tests or school reports are the raw data of the psychiatric evaluation. The professional then draws from these her notion of what triggers the problem in a given family's environment, as well as her impressions of a child's particular sensitivities. She assesses the stress management styles of the parents: How do they respond when their child's upset, and why do they respond this way, based on their personalities and their pasts? She has also gotten a look at how the child handles anger and where things stand regarding the development of a legacy.

Next, parents and child return for a meeting with

the therapist in which she goes over her findings and recommends a treatment plan. Ideally, especially if the child is old enough, everyone should take part in this meeting. It needn't be an occasion for the therapist to issue a unilateral decree. If everyone has a say in how the treatment will proceed, it establishes a good model for open, honest work together.

Parents may wonder exactly what kinds of treatment there are for anger problems. There's a wide range of remedies depending upon the problem and its severity. For example, a therapist may simply offer advice to the parents about certain things that trigger anger in the child, and how the parents might change these. He might offer guidance on how to help a child navigate a particularly rough passage in her life. Then he could request that the parents check back with him after a certain period.

In other cases, a professional might recommend that the parents undergo extended counseling for their own marital conflicts, the way they handle their child's anger, or other individual problems that they need to work through. They may need help because they have doubts about their parenting abilities and their own anger, and they need the support of an objective presence.

If the child exhibits a well-established legacy, some sort of intensive psychotherapy is usually necessary. This may involve the child having individual sessions with the therapist, combined with the parents regularly visiting the therapist for feedback and counseling. Family psychotherapy, in which everyone is present and the focus is on the family unit, could be suggested from the beginning. Sometimes individual and family therapy are combined in different ways.

Another possibility is that a parent or parents and their child will receive therapy together, such as mother-child conjoint therapy. Alternatively, a therapist may recommend that a parent alone receive intensive counseling. The hope in such instances is that the therapist's work with the parent will lead directly to changes in how a mother or father relates to a son or daughter. With infants, of course, parent-child treatment is always the rule.

In cases in which a parent's anger is out of control or in which the parents have deep-seated legacies of their own, it's common for a therapist to recommend that the parents pursue their own intensive treatment. Obviously, a parent's successful treatment can have a highly beneficial effect on his or her children's future.

Occasionally, a therapist may find anger problems in a family so out of control that it seems beneficial for the child to spend some time away from home, at least temporarily. In other cases, the therapist might consult with personnel at the child's school, or suggest that the child be put on a medication.

Whatever treatment you and you child embark upon, remember that you ought to see results after a certain period of time. These don't come overnight, any more than the problems did. However, it's good to ask for realistic expectations regarding behavioral and emotional changes, and a time when you might reasonably begin to notice these. Such questions can't be answered precisely, especially not at the very beginning of treatment, but it's reasonable to ask them, and the therapist ought to be able to give you some answers in due time.

When people of any age understand that angry feelings express a need for help, anger automatically loses much of its power and mystery and becomes less frightening. The defenses that we've built against it begin to seem unnecessary and, ultimately, they melt away. Letting go of these defenses dismantles the process of anger metamorphosis. Since it's the engine that's been driving the child's psychiatric disturbance, that disappears as well.

This isn't magic. It takes courage, a commitment to change, time, and hard work, but I've seen it happen again and again.

Angry feelings needn't be the enemy. Understanding this fact is the starting point in helping our kids to handle these feelings in a healthy way. Anger is simply one among many emotions, and it is natural, normal, and appropriate. It's something that we can learn to treasure in our children rather than deplore. If we're able to do that, we will have given them a gift that will stand them in good stead for the rest of their lives.

## PROFESSIONAL HELP GUIDELINES

- Professional help is often not needed. If you have become knowledgeable about your child's anger expression and have learned how to locate its source and intervene, then there is no need for help.
- Don't be shy about getting some professional guidance even if you don't see a big problem. Sometimes a little counseling can help avoid major problems later on.
- Think of seeking advice if you are unsure of yourself regarding anger because of your own past unresolved anger issues.
- If you see forerunners of legacy behavior, not yet full-blown, but not understandable either, seek advice.
- Certain situations make help mandatory, and include the presence of a full-blown legacy of mishandled anger or the danger of a parent committing child abuse.
- Professional credentials, references, and your gut reaction to a therapist are your best guidelines for making the correct choice.

# Conclusion

My purpose in writing this book is to convey the message that angry feelings are as vital to youngsters as any other emotion, and that the way angry feelings are handled makes a great difference in how a child develops.

Angry kids aren't easy for any of us. Their feelings can trigger painful memories, remind us of unresolved issues about our relationships with our own parents, and immerse us in confusion—our own and society's—about anger. Children's angry feelings also make us confront the ways in which we mishandle our own anger, how this has affected our lives, and how it's now affecting our children.

Most people reading this book will be able to get a handle on the anger issues their kids present. A few particularly salient points will be helpful to remember.

- A child's anger should be considered a normal expression of distress and helplessness that can come from a wide variety of circumstances.

- Anger expression follows some general patterns, but it's crucial to be familiar with your child's unique ways of showing angry feelings.
- Assume that, as a human being, you have some preconceived notions about anger that may interfere with your responding objectively to your child's anger. Get acquainted with your own anger biases and attempt to overcome them.
- Unless a child's anger endangers her or someone else, focus on understanding its source rather than lecturing, chastising, or punishing the child. Patient observation, compassionate questioning, and sensitive listening are the tools that lead to understanding.
- After locating the anger's source, remember that your objective is to relieve the distress that's causing the anger.
- You'll probably be able to handle most situations involving anger and your child. Sometimes professional aid is helpful, and often it's simply brief, educational counseling. If one of the legacies of mishandled anger has developed, outside help is mandatory, as it is if you feel that you're out of control and could harm your child.

Life itself causes a certain amount of natural pain, suffering, and anger in all of us—that's its nature. I'm convinced that if children's anger is handled constructively—if adults appreciate and understand that mad kids aren't bad ones—the lives that result will be free of major, crippling problems. Every parent wants that for his or her child. If our culture as a whole adopted a similar appreciation of anger, we might even begin moving toward a cure for the scourge of symptomatic violence that has afflicted our society for so long.